cocktails

shaken and stirred

Winner of 'Mixologist of the year 2001' and countless other accolades, Douglas Ankrah is a leading figure in the international bar scene and is considered to be one of the main instigators of London's cocktail revolution of the 90s.

If you haven't heard of Douglas Ankrah you may have heard of his award-winning London bars: Lab and Townhouse.

After many years behind bars (including The Hard Rock, Planet Hollywood and Dick's Bar) Douglas and a friend co-founded the London Academy of Bartenders (LAB) in 1996, where they trained personnel for many of London's best-known bars. This lead to the opening of their own, groundbreaking, cocktail bar Lab, in 1999.

Lab soon became recognised as one of London's most innovative bars, and has been credited with revolutionising London's bar scene. It went on to win a multitude of awards including *Time Out* Bar of the Year 2000, Flavour Cocktail Bar of the Year 2002, and '26th Best Bar in the World' in *The Independent's* top 50 bars in the world.

In 2002 Douglas opened Townhouse, his boutique bar concept, on Beauchamp Place, Knightsbridge. Townhouse was soon given the accolade of being the '10th most Stylish Thing About London' by *Time Out* and has also gone on to win many awards including Flavour Bar of the Year 2003.

When he's not opening bars Douglas is developing new drinks and discovering new flavours both for his own bars and also as a consultant for some of the world's biggest drinks companies. He is in great demand as a bar consultant and has consulted on many bars and restaurants across the world from London to Japan to Dubai.

DOUGLAS ANKRAH

Cocktails
Shaken and Stirred
by Douglas Ankrah

Photographs by Lisa Linder

Kyle Cathie Limited

First published in Great Britain in 2004 by Kyle Cathie Limited
122 Arlington Road, London NW1 7HP
www.kylecathie.com

This edition published in 2007

10 9 8 7 6 5 4 3 2 1

ISBN 978 1 85626 727 4

Douglas Ankrah is hereby identified as the author of this work in accordance with Section 77 of the Copyright, Designs and Patents Act 1988.

Text copyright © 2004 Douglas Ankrah
Photography copyright © 2004 Lisa Linder except for pp 120, 127, 128–129, 130
Book design © 2004 Kyle Cathie Limited

Editor: Sophie Allen
Design and Art Direction: Susanna Cook of Allies
Photography: Lisa Linder
Home Economist: Robert Reed
Stylist: Lucinda Maydon
Indexer: Alex Corrin
Production: Sha Huxtable & Alice Holloway

A Cataloguing In Publication record for this title is available from the British Library.

Colour reproduction by Scanhouse,
Printed and bound by Tien Wah Press, Singapore

Acknowledgements:

A very special thanks to my mum, Theodora. Thanks for all your support and for handling me with care. This book is dedicated to you.

Thanks to Ms Ewa Helwich for all her assistance and hard work during the photo shoots for the book – the lady bartender in London...
Robert Reed: your food creations truly match my drink creations, and for being patient...
Michael and Catherine Mckenna for the jewellery, Isabella Kristensen for that sexy dress on the front cover...
All at Kyle Cathie for giving Shaken & Stirred a chance and to Bill Knott...
Big thanks to Graham Syme for all his help over the years.

Picture Acknowledgements
120 right, Karen Marchant, General Manager of Duke's Hotel; 127 El Floridita; 128 right, Victor Bergeron, 129, Patrons dining at Trader Vic's, Time Life Pictures/Getty Images; 130 bond girls. clockwise from top left: Miss Moneypenny and Bond, Goldfinger; Pussy Galore, Goldfinger; Bibi Dahl, For Your Eyes Only (ph Keith Hamshere); Holly Goodhead, Moonraker (ph Patrick Morin); May Day, A View to a Kill; Jinx, Die Another Day (ph Keith Hamshere); Tiffany Case, Diamonds are Forever; Kissy Suzuki, You Only Live Twice; Honey Rider, Doctor No; Christmas Jones, The World is Not Enough (ph Keith Hamshere); all Danjaq/Eon/UA, courtesy of Kobal Collection.

Special thanks to these companies for their generosity in lending items for the Entertaining at Home section:- Babylon Design, Ceramica Blue, The Conran Shop, The Cross, Harrods, Inwater, Liberty, Muji, Musa, Ozwald Boateng, Paul Smith, Tom McEwan for his gorgeous jewels (bond girls section), Steiner of Visionary Living for his fabulous flowers and vases.

All cocktail recipes serve 2 people, unless stated otherwise.

Contents

Introduction

What is a cocktail? A dictionary might tell you that it is a mixed drink, often iced, flavoured and sweetened, and based on a spirit of some kind.

While that might be literally true – and indeed is true of most of the cocktails in this book – a cocktail is much more than that to me. It is creativity, skill and flair in a glass. It can create a special atmosphere just by being lovingly made and attractively served; even before customers in my bar have taken a sip, I can sometimes feel their mood changing.

It is not simply an alcoholic mish-mash. During Prohibition, it is true that many mixed drinks were made from inferior ingredients, and some cocktails were designed to conceal bathtub gin or some other unspeakable hooch. Nowadays, however, there is no excuse for using inferior spirits: even in the unlikely event that you can disguise them with ice and flavourings, there will be no disguising your hangover the next morning.

This book is the culmination of my experiences of shaking, muddling, mixing and straining drinks professionally for the last 15 years. It is not just a handbook for bartenders, however, it is a guide to reproducing at home some of the drinks you would normally find only in smart cocktail bars.

When I create a new cocktail, I often find my inspiration – like, I think, a musician might – from the people and things around me: a song on the radio, the people I meet, the places I visit, the smell of a garden… any stimuli, really, that get the creative juices flowing.

I always try to create drinks that look stunning and taste fantastic – a perfect drink should be the perfect colour. I love the mechanics of making a new cocktail, and the theatrical aspect of conjuring up cocktails at the bar, but the biggest kick I get is from a delighted customer.

My aim in writing this book was to demystify the whole process of mixing cocktails; at the same time, I wanted to give a real sense of the fun and energy on which the best bars thrive. This, I hope, is a stylish book to read and enjoy, as well as a friendly, no-nonsense guide to making the best drinks possible.

Some of the cocktails are straightforward, others take a little more skill and patience, but they are all achievable, and if you derive even half the pleasure from mixing them as I have from creating them, then I'll be happy.

Take your time over making cocktails: not so long that the ice melts, but enough to plan carefully what ingredients and equipment you will need. It's easier in a bar because you have all the ingredients to hand, but at home you really have the time to perfect each drink. If you are having a party, just choose 2 or 3 drinks that you are confident making. Think about the garnish: it is often said that people eat with their eyes. I think they drink with them too.

Experiment, especially once you have mastered the basics. Taste everything you make, even for other people. Is it too strong? Too weak? Too sweet? Too bitter? Many faults can be corrected immediately, with an extra drop or two of gomme syrup, lemon juice or bitters: if not, at least you will know better next time. Experiment, too, with different fruits: many of the recipes in the book can be altered to suit whatever is available. Much better to make a slightly different drink using fruit that is in season, rather than slavishly follow a recipe using frozen or tinned fruit.

Skill and flair take a little practice, but the creativity is inside you already. Happy shaking, happy stirring and happy drinking!

Glassware

Hugely important to the success of any cocktail is the right choice of glass. Serve a Martini in a highball glass, or a Negroni in a Martini glass, and you will see what I mean. It just doesn't work.

One thing to bear in mind is the strength of the drink: a long drink made with soda or Coke – a Mojito for example – often needs a taller glass than a short, strong drink like an Old Fashioned. A small surface area at the top of the drink helps to keep a fizzy drink bubbling; a bigger surface area can help flavours to develop in the glass, as with an Old Fashioned. The volume of a drink – the amount of liquid – is also, obviously, important in deciding the correct glass to use.

Some glasses, like the Martini glass, are designed for a cold drink without rocks of ice; others, like a highball, are perfect for a gin and tonic. I have recommended a particular glass for each of the cocktails in the book, but if you start to experiment – as I hope you will – with your own drinks, then bear in mind the ideas I've outlined here before you choose which glass to serve them in.

Consider also whether you will serve it with a straw, how the glass will help or hinder the presentation of your cocktail, and – most importantly, because you need to think ahead – whether you want the glass to be frozen: Martinis are much better in really cold glasses. Try to keep a few Martini glasses and a few shot glasses in the freezer, just in case.

The key glasses used are:-

Highball — a tall glass used for long drinks.

Old-fashioned — a short, sturdy glass ideal for serving scotch on the rocks, or a spirit with a small top-up of mixer.

Champagne Flute — currently the most widely used glass for Champagne and Champagne cocktails.

Shot — designed for drinks consumed in one go.

Martini 5oz — a straight-sided classic glass with a long stem to prevent the drink warming up. Best for a classic gin or vodka Martini.

Martini 7oz — good for weaker, fruit-based Martinis.

Goblet – large, stemmed glass (a double wine glass) ideal for 'fancy' cocktails.

Brandy Balloon – elegant glass usually containing a double measure.

Equipment

Lots of different equipment is available to the cocktail aficionado, but you can make most of the drinks in this book without investing hundreds of pounds in state-of-the-art tools.

One thing you really should invest in, however, is a Boston shaker, which comes in 2 halves: a toughened glass, which forms a perfect seal, with a stainless steel cup that is slightly wider at the rim, allowing the 2 halves to be sharply rapped together and safely shaken, without redecorating your kitchen in fruit and alcohol.

A Hawthorn strainer is a useful investment: you could use a small sieve to achieve the same results, but the Hawthorn fits neatly over a Boston glass and is perfect for keeping ice out of drinks.

Professional blenders tend to be a little sturdier and have bigger motors than domestic versions, but your home liquidiser will be fine for most blended drinks. Just be careful not to use hard cubed ice: it will not crack properly and may well break the motor. Use crushed ice instead, or pour over rocks after blending.

A mixing glass is used for stirring cocktails with ice – a Martini, for example. It tends to be larger than a Boston glass, but either will do.

A good sized ice bucket is also handy, with tongs for hard ice cubes and a small scoop for crushed ice.

Aside from that, the usual bottle openers and corkscrews are handy: the Waiter's (or Barman's) Friend is the simplest and best.

Bar spoons are really just long-handled teaspoons, used for stirring tall glasses or occasionally for light muddling duties: bruising mint leaves or lime leaves, for instance. It can also be used for layering shooters, or for floats.

Free-pouring is much easier using pourers: they are cork and chrome spouts that fit in the bottle's neck and provide a thin, constant stream of drink. They also help with the theatrical aspect of cocktail making – if that is something that appeals!

A muddler is essential for extracting the juice from fruit and for bruising mint leaves and bashing other herbs. Most are wooden and look a little like small rolling pins.

Measures are useful even at home: they will help you achieve the right proportions in your creations. Standard UK measures are 25ml and 50ml. They will also help you learn to free-pour: that is, to pour accurate measures by eye, a skill all good cocktail makers need.

A fine strainer or tea strainer is useful, especially for drinks with lots of pulp or pips.

A good, sharp knife and a small chopping board are vital for cleanly prepared, appetising garnishes.

Methods

Stirring

If you don't have a mixing glass, you can use the Boston glass. Fill up your mixing glass with cubed ice then add the spirit and the liqueur, stir with a bar spoon or a dessert spoon. Classic drinks like a Martini are made in this way.

Layering

Most layered drinks are made in shot glasses and usually consist of liqueurs as they float better. To layer or float a liquid pour over the back of a barspoon (or a teaspoon) into the glass.

Blending

Blended drinks can be a nightmare to make. If you can, use crushed ice or simply put about 8–10 ice cubes in a large tea towel and bash them until evenly crushed. Make sure you use the correct measures so the drinks blend well with the ice. Blend for about 20 seconds and use ripe fruit.

Pouring

When making drinks, make sure you pour the correct amount. Too much alcohol will ruin the drink. Example: when making a gin and tonic, make sure the highball glass is filled with cubed ice then add your gin then the tonic, finally stir it really well and then garnish.

Shaking

The aim of shaking a cocktail is to make sure that the drink you are planning to serve is both cold and thoroughly mixed. It can also introduce air into the drink, which can give a slightly frothy texture to some cocktails, especially cream-based drinks. The Boston shaker is made up of 2 pieces, the Boston glass and the metal mixing tin. Pour your ingredients into the ice filled Boston glass, as this allows you to see the amount of spirits and liqueurs you're using for the drink. The mixing tin acts as a base, and is the right volume for 2 drinks. Shake for about 10-15 seconds, enough time to dissolve sugar into spirit. The metal of the shaker should be freezing cold by the time you have finished; finally, strain the cocktail and discard the ice.

Muddling

Muddling involves crushing fruit, herbs (usually mint) and sometimes sugar together to create a flavoursome residue. Drinks like the Caipirinha and Mojito are muddled in a heavy or toughened Old-fashioned glass.

Bashing

Usually you bash herbs or some fruits (like watermelon) to break them up and release the flavour. You can use a muddler or rolling pin.

Ice

Just as anyone learning to cook needs to understand what heat does to food, so any aspiring cocktail-maker needs to know how ice affects drinks. Ice is vital both for making and for serving cocktails, and it can make a huge difference to the success of a drink.

When cocktails started being popular again in Britain, a lot of customers, used to the flimsy remnants of ice in the bucket on the bar in their local, were surprised at the sheer quantity of ice used by good bartenders. Old-fashioned glasses were filled with rocks of hard ice, highballs were filled to the brim with crushed ice and 2 myths about ice emerged. The first is that cocktail bars fill glasses with ice because ice is cheap. In any good bar, this is simply untrue. You can ask for less ice in a drink if you like, but that does not mean you will get more of everything else: it simply means your drink will be less successful. Which brings us to myth number 2: that the more ice a drink contains, the more dilute it will be. In fact, a glass filled with ice stays much colder than a glass with only a little ice: be stingy with the ice, and it will simply melt into the drink.

An iced cocktail should still have plenty of ice in the glass when the drink has been finished: if it doesn't, it should either have had more (or colder) ice to start with, or it should have been drunk more quickly.

Speed of consumption is up to you, but the ice should at least keep the drink cold for 15 minutes or so.

For practical purposes at home, there are 2 sorts of ice: hard ice cubes and crushed ice. Hard ice cubes can either be made in the freezer or bought in bags: actually, homemade ice cubes, made in generously sized trays, are better than most of the ice you can buy in bags. The cubes are larger, with less relative surface area, so they are slower to melt. Buy a few trays, empty the ice into plastic bags when frozen, refill the trays and you will quickly build up a good supply of top-quality hard ice.

Crushed ice is more of a problem. If you are lucky enough to have a fridge-freezer that makes it for you, that's perfect; if not, you will have to bash hard ice wrapped in a tea towel to crush it or invest in an ice crusher.

Lastly, remember that a frozen glass will keep both the drink and its ice much colder than one at room temperature or (heaven forbid) a warm glass. Keeping a selection of glasses in the freezer is a good idea; generally, a well stocked freezer is the key to making good cocktails at home.

Garnishing

Fashion in garnishing drinks changes almost as often as fashions in ladies' hats; in fact, in the 80s, hats and cocktails looked rather similar.

The classic garnishes – the olive in a Martini or the cherry in a Manhattan – are really part of the drink: small, reasonably discreet and rather elegant, adding a complementary or contrasting flavour or aroma to the cocktail.

From the 70s, however, drinks started to change. Piña Coladas and Tequila Sunrises started to be served with theatrical pizazz in hollowed-out coconuts or pineapples, overwhelmed with exotic fruit, gaudily coloured mini umbrellas and sparklers until the drink itself was barely noticeable.

Such pyrotechnic miracles of the bartender's art are still available in various corners of the globe, mostly next to swimming pools in tropical holiday resorts, but elsewhere a more restrained approach has taken hold.

The point of a garnish is to enhance the drink, not to overwhelm it. As with food, the idea is both to please the eye and to give the palate an idea of what to expect. Why chefs ever thought that a scratchy sprig of parsley made their creation more attractive is difficult to understand; similarly, a moribund lemon slice or a gratuitous cherry adds nothing to a drink.

Use your imagination too; if you are making a drink with elderflower cordial, for example, and you have elderflowers in the garden, then use them, or perhaps try a fresh bay leaf in a martini. Cocktail bars do not, as a rule, have herb or fruit gardens, so make the most of your advantage and personalise your drinks.

When a recipe calls for, say, a dozen raspberries, make sure you save the best examples to top the drink; similarly, mint bashed in a Mojito does not have to be of pristine quality, but the sprig on top should be fresh and bright green.

A sharp knife and a good little chopping board are essential for garnishes: sharp, clean cuts look attractive and help to stop garnishes from discolouring.

These are the best ways of garnishing cocktails:

Lemon and lime wedges – top and tail, cut in half lengthways and then cut each half into 3–4 wedges, depending on size. Choose attractive fruit with evenly coloured skin for garnishing: less beautiful examples can be used for juicing.

Lemon, lime and orange twists – these are long strips of zest: the idea is to make use of the citrus oils in the skin, which give an inimitable aroma to drinks. The pith, by contrast, is bitter and needs to be trimmed off. Top and tail the fruit, then carefully pare a strip from the skin all the way from top to bottom – about 1.5cm (2/3 in) wide for an orange, 1cm (1/2 in) for a lemon and a little less for a lime. Turn it pith-side up on a chopping board and, holding it with thumb and forefinger, carefully saw away the pith until you can see just the colour of the fruit. The twist will now add flavour from both sides, with no bitterness.

Lemon, lime and kiwi fruit wheels – use the best examples you can find and slice across the widest part of the fruit into rounds, about 0.5cm (1/4 in) wide. You can then cut from the peel to the centre so that the wheel will perch easily on the rim of a glass.

Pineapple wedges – top and tail a fresh pineapple, cut lengthways into quarters, remove the core (which can be tough, but is also sweet and can be cut into chunks and juiced). Each quarter can now be laid sideways on a board and cut into slices 1cm (1/2 in) thick, then cut into wedges.

Pineapple leaves – just pick a few of the best looking leaves off the top of a pineapple and slide them onto the rim of the glass.

Orange and lemon slices – top and tail the orange and cut in half lengthways. Place the cut side down on a chopping board and slice into 1cm (1/2 in) wide half moons. Cut a short slit in the flesh if you want to perch it on the rim of the glass.

Celery – wash and trim the celery; if the sticks seem especially stringy, take a potato peeler and pare off the string from the outside of the stalk. Cut them in half lengthways if they are very wide and trim them so that they will just poke out of the glass. Long celery sticks have been known to get up drinkers' noses. Literally…

Olives – a wide variety of olives can be found in delis and supermarkets, green, black, dried black, Kalamata, and stuffed green, to name a few. For cocktails, large, unstuffed, stoned green olives are the classic, but you might experiment with pimento- almond- or even anchovy-stuffed green olives.

Maraschino cherries – you either love them or hate them, but they have a strong, sweet almond/cherry flavour and should be used with discretion.

Pearl onions – the classic garnish which turns a Martini into a Gibson: 2 pearl onions speared on a cocktail stick. A dash of the vinegary juice makes a Martini a Dirty Martini.

Strawberries – the bigger and more beautiful the better for garnishing: use any slightly squashy, small or unattractive specimens for juicing or muddling. Leave on the green leafy top if it looks good and carefully slit the bottom of the berry so it can cling to the rim.

Mint – fresh green mint is really important, for flavour as well as looks. Look for springy bunches with thin red stalks and a bright, pale green colour; even better, grow it in your garden – it is a very hardy little herb.

Banana slices – slice the banana diagonally into 1cm (1/2 in) thick slices, rub with a little lemon juice and slit from skin to centre to hold it to the rim of a glass. Leaving the skin on is sensible.

Cucumber slices – leave the skin on for garnishing a Pimm's, peel it for a paler drink and slice straight across or diagonally, according to aesthetic taste and the size of your cucumber. Slices should be about 0.5cm (1/4 in) wide.

Apple fans – cut a section from one side of a crisp green or red apple, lay it flat on a board, slice off both ends and then cut into 5 or 6 neat, thin slices. Carefully skewer all the slices at one end with a toothpick, then fan out into a sort of Sydney Opera House arrangement and dust with a mixture of icing sugar and ground cinnamon. You can also make pear fans, lemon fans, strawberry fans and mango fans.

Lemongrass tubes – cut the lemongrass about a third of the way up. Open out the layers and they should naturally curve back into little tubes that you insert into the drink.

Straws – obviously these are used to drink the cocktail, but they can also be

Vodka

Vodka has one great advantage for making cocktails: it is more or less flavourless, giving it the ability to blend harmoniously with any other flavour. Its main purpose is simply to add alcoholic strength to a cocktail.

There are exceptions to this rule: the Vodka Martini, for example, in which the delicate aromas, the level of oiliness and the dryness of the finish are vital. You might choose a premium brand for a Martini, like Grey Goose or Ketel One.

For other cocktails, any good quality vodka will probably suffice: as a general rule, there is little point in paying extra for a subtly flavoured spirit only to mask its expensive nuances with stronger flavours. Very cheap vodkas, however, are best avoided, unless you particularly relish hangovers.

Flavoured vodkas have been around for centuries, usually drunk simply as 'shots', but have become increasingly popular in mixed drinks. Companies like Wyborowa, Stolichnaya and Absolut have introduced dozens of new flavours: some are better than others and you might like to compare a few before you buy.

One flavoured vodka with a longer history than most is Zubrowka, a Polish vodka flavoured with bison grass. Poles tend to drink it either cold and neat, or with apple juice. The grass itself grows wild in the meadows of the Bialowieska forest, in eastern Poland, an area much frequented by the only herd of bison in Europe. The survival of the herd is allegedly due to the grass acting as an aphrodisiac.

Vodka translates as 'dear little water' in Russia, where (as in many countries in Eastern Europe and central Asia) it is the national drink. Fermented grain or potatoes are distilled to produce a relatively neutral spirit, a process carried out in Russia since the late 9th Century, and perhaps even earlier in Poland. In fact, since all vodka relies on is a source of readily fermentable carbohydrate, it can be made from almost anything: rice and molasses are also used.

Gin

Gin has a long and somewhat chequered history. The classic flavouring is dried juniper berries and most sources seem to think that the Dutch (who still drink various kinds of jenever) invented it, although the Italians also have a claim, perhaps because Italy has traditionally been the source for juniper.

The only gin worth buying is one in which the 'gin head' is employed: a method of distilling the spirit with the botanicals to create subtle and well balanced flavours. Cheaper and cruder methods simply involve adding flavourings, or macerating the spirit with botanicals. None of the well known brands employs these techniques, although dubiously labelled gins made in Asia or Africa almost certainly do.

Like many spirits and liqueurs, gin started life as a medicine, with claims made for its efficacy in treating dozens of complaints, ranging from gout to gallstones. By the 18th Century, however, the popularity of cheap, badly distilled gin in London and other cities had led to the sort of social breakdown famously lampooned by Hogarth in his etching 'Gin Lane'. Distribution was controlled, taxes were raised, and the English went back to beer.

Two styles of gin are officially recognised: London and Plymouth, differing mainly in the botanicals employed in their manufacture. London gin tends to favour juniper while, in Plymouth gin, orris root is a dominant aroma. Other gins are now available with a variety of not-so-traditional flavourings: try Hendrick's gin, flavoured with cucumber and rose petals, or Tanqueray No.10, which employs fresh botanicals in the gin head instead of the usual dried herbs, roots and spices.

Strength is an important factor with gin: alcohol content ranges from 37.5% ABV for Gordon's to 47.3% for Tanqueray No.10, a vital consideration when mixing a Martini. Lower strength gins might be better straight from the freezer, higher strength gins stirred with ice, but it really depends on personal preference. You may well find that your favourite brand of gin for a Martini is different from your favourite to mix with tonic. Happy experiments, however, are assured.

Tequila

Before Cortes and his Spanish conquistadores toppled the Aztec kingdom in Mexico, locals had grown rather fond of a milky, slightly sour cactus 'beer' called pulque.

While pulquerias still survive in Mexico, the technology that the Spanish brought with them allowed them to distil pulque into a spirit, known as tequila and now Mexico's national drink. Tequila is actually a sort of mezcal, with production restricted to the Jalisco region around Guadalajara and the town Tequila, where the best variety of blue agave cactus thrives.

As with any spirit, what comes out of the still is a clear liquid at high proof. It can then either be bottled as it is, darkened with caramel to give an illusion of age (often called simply 'gold'), or actually aged in wood, which mellows the spirit and adds notes of vanilla and other spices to the drink: añejo and reposado are the two terms which guarantee a wood-aged tequila.

Its assertive flavour is difficult, but not impossible, to balance in cocktails, which is perhaps why the classic methods of shots and slammers are most popular. Mexicans themselves tend to use salt, chilli and lime to accompany cheaper versions, but a really good barrel-aged tequila can be sipped like malt whisky or a fine dark rum.

Rum

Chemically speaking, sugar cane is the easiest and most efficient crop to ferment and then distil and countries in which sugar cane grows have taken full advantage of the fact. Rum is made all over the Caribbean and Central America.

Rum's history is inextricably and romantically linked with pirates, buccaneering on the high seas and tots of grog, and less happily with the slave trade. The sugar cane plantations originally used slave labour, and slaves were regularly traded for rum.

Either the juice or the molasses from sugar cane is fermented to produce a clear spirit, then, as with tequila, the result can either be bottled as white rum, or aged, often with caramel or molasses added to intensify colour.

Both Bacardi and Havana Club produce a range of rums from white to dark and wood-aged: white rum is perhaps best suited to a Mojito, its young and powerful flavour ideally matched with mint, lime and sugar, while the rich aroma and flavour of darker rums are better suited to mellower combinations: soft summer fruits, for example. The best rums need nothing but a snifter, especially the artisanal rums from Martinique (look for the word 'Agricole') and Haiti.

Wray & Nephew rum from Jamaica is reputed to have medicinal properties: local people use it as a cure for headaches or flu. The method involves applying a rum-soaked cloth to the forehead, although drinking it may prove equally efficacious.

Scotch whisky

The Scottish may not have been the first to make whisky – that distinction probably belongs to the Irish – but Scotch whisky is now the most famous and widely available spirit in the world.

The best Scotch is made from malted barley, roasted over a peat fire, fermented, then distilled in a pot still, and aged in wood for 8 years or more, when it can be sold as 'single malt'. Cheaper Scotch uses a proportion of lighter flavoured grain whisky in a blend with malt whisky, hence the term 'blended'.

Some blended whiskies, however, are perfect for cocktails – J&B Rare is a good example – whereas the distinctively peaty malts from Islay – Lagavulin, for instance – are best drunk on their own; indeed, making a Whisky Sour with Islay malt is probably a hanging offence in the Western Isles.

All Scotch is, to a greater or lesser extent, peaty, since at least some of the malt is roasted in an open kiln: in Ireland, the kiln is closed, so Irish whiskey (with an 'e') is traditionally unpeaty. The Irish also distil 3 times rather than twice, in theory making a smoother drink. Any cocktail specifying Scotch can be made equally successfully with Irish whiskey.

The huge international popularity of Scotch whisky has led many countries to make their own, with varying results: the best, surprisingly, are the Japanese, whose Suntory whiskeys are very well made. The latest entrant in the international whisky stakes is India: Amrut whisky is made with malt grown in the foothills of the Himalayas and distilled in Bangalore. The optimistic distillers plan to sell it, amongst other places, in Scottish curry houses.

Bourbon

Despite its all-American image, Bourbon actually owes its existence to Scottish whisky makers: a group of immigrant Scots started making whisky in Kentucky in the 18th century using maize, a crop better suited to local conditions than the barley they had used at home.

Bourbon is instantly identifiable as different from malt whisky; the corn gives a sweetness to the nose and palate, while the charred oak barrels used for maturation give it a smoky aroma and strong hints of vanilla.

At its best, bourbon stands comparison with the finest single malts, especially single batch bourbons, often bottled at cask strength. Less rarified bourbons – Maker's Mark and Woodford Reserve, for instance – are perfect for cocktails, with pronounced flavours that marry well with orange zest, summer fruits and warm spices. The vanilla component in bourbon can be easily enhanced by inserting a slit vanilla pod into the bottle.

Jack Daniel's, a very similar whiskey to bourbon, is actually from neighbouring Tennessee and is known as 'Tennessee Sour Mash', it can be used in any cocktail recipe that specifies bourbon.

The Store Cupboard

The cocktail kitchen has much in common with any other kitchen: it relies on fresh ingredients, especially fruit, but it also needs a store cupboard full of basics.

We have already discussed spirits that are essential for your store cupboard, and, by making some of the cocktails in this book, you will gradually accumulate a stock of liqueurs. As well as these, however, you might find the following list useful.

Vermouth – red (sweet) and white (dry) vermouths are indispensable in a whole host of cocktails. Vya, from California, and Noilly Prat, from France, are the two most famous premium brands. Both make both red and white, although the Noilly Prat red can be hard to find. Martini Extra Dry and Martini Rosso are widely available.

Bitters – Angostura bitters are essential: if you are a fan of bitters-flavoured drinks, you might want to invest in bottles of orange or peach bitters.
Worcestershire sauce is vital for a Bloody Mary, or any tomato-based cocktail, as is Tabasco.

Garnishes – jars of maraschino cherries, olives and silverskin onions are easy to store in the fridge or the cupboard. Fruit garnishes need to be fresh, and should be bought as needed, but keeping a few lemons and limes in the fridge or the fruitbowl is a good idea if you need an emergency cocktail. Supermarkets often sell fruit when it is not yet ripe, so it is often best to buy fresh fruit a couple of days before you want to use it so you can ripen it properly; this will improve your cocktails no end.

Gomme Syrup – sugar syrup – features in many of the recipes in this book. It has the advantage of already being dissolved, so it can be stirred or shaken into a drink very easily. To make your own, heat 600ml (1 pint) of water, and once it is boiling add 1kg (2^1/4lb) sugar, and boil until it becomes a thick syrup – about 10–15 minutes. Add more water if it becomes too thick. Remove any scum from the top, allow to cool and funnel into clean bottles. Otherwise, buy it from any good cocktail-friendly off-licence.

Sugars – The other sugars it helps to have are caster and soft brown sugar, both cheap and easy to find, and vanilla sugar, which can either be bought, or made at home. To make it blend 3 fresh vanilla pods with 1kg (2^1/4lb) caster sugar. Once blended sieve to catch some of the larger black pieces. Store in an airtight container.

Honey – acacia or any runny honey are best – is useful, as is a good espresso coffee, celery salt and cans or packets of coconut cream. Ground cinnamon and whole nutmeg also come in handy for dusting over garnishes or creamy drinks.

Juices and sodas – juices are best made or bought fresh: in any case, long life juices rarely make a good drink. An exception is cranberry juice, which is usually long life and actually a 'juice drink', with water and added sugar. Also, good quality canned or long life tomato juice can make a decent Bloody Mary.

Tonic water, soda water, lemonade (7-Up for preference) and ginger beer (Fentiman's is best) are always useful: try to find cans, rather than huge bottles. It may work out a little more expensive, but nothing dulls a drink more than flat tonic or soda water.

Fruit purées – specialist shops now sell a good range of frozen fruit purées, which are excellent for cocktails. What you want to stock in your freezer will depend on your favourite drinks: Bellini fans will look for frozen peach purée, while aficionados of the fruity Martini might go for passionfruit, raspberries or blackberries.
You can, of course, make your own: almost any berry can be cooked with a little sugar, puréed, strained, and frozen in ice cube trays. Here are recipes for passionfruit and raspberry.

Passionfruit purée
14 ripe passionfruit
300ml water
500g caster sugar
Scoop the flesh out of the passionfruit and blend. Boil the water and then add the sugar and passionfruit until the mixture becomes a thick syrup – about 10–15 minutes. Strain and leave to cool, then either bottle and store in the fridge or put it in a bag in the freezer.

Raspberry purée
2 punnets fresh raspberries
100ml gomme syrup
Blend the raspberries with the gomme syrup. Push through a sieve so that the syrup is smooth.

Flavoured vodkas – if you don't want to splash out on flavoured vodkas, it is easy to make your own. The most useful is raspberry flavoured vodka, which is easy to make and gives the bland taste of vodka a delicious twist.

Raspberry-flavoured vodka
Insert 12 fresh raspberries to a nearly full bottle of vodka, and 1 tablespoon of gomme syrup, and leave for 4–5 days. Strain to remove the raspberries, otherwise they will ferment and ruin the flavour. Store in the fridge or freezer.

Vanilla-flavoured vodka
Split 2 fresh vanilla pods into 2, then insert the pods into a nearly full bottle of vodka. Add 50ml of gomme syrup and leave for about 4–5 days. Strain and store in the fridge or freezer.

Breezes, Collinses and Martinis

The Breeze

The Sea Breeze is a favourite with bartenders, because it is so quick and easy to make. At home, it's a perfect party drink: you don't really want to be shaking Martinis for 24 people. Try one of the variations on the theme for a more original crowd-pleaser.

The Collins

These days, the Collins is perhaps best known as a forerunner of the Mojito, which is really just a Collins made with rum. However you drink it, a Collins is the perfect drink before lunch on a sunny day. For the Collins' variations you can use gin or vodka.

The New Martini

The purist will tell you – quite rightly – that just because a drink is in a Martini glass doesn't make it a Martini. Strictly speaking, a Martini is made with gin, not vodka (which makes a Vodkatini), and is flavoured just with a dash of vermouth.

Rules are made to be broken, however, and a new generation of Martinis has sprung up, mostly flavoured with fresh fruit and considerably less punchy than the traditional versions. Four of any of these, and Dorothy Parker might just have avoided ending up under the host.

Summer Breeze

A sort of distillation of the English summer.

2 Highball glasses

100ml Grey Goose orange vodka (or Absolut Mandrin)
25ml elderflower cordial
100ml cloudy apple juice
100ml cranberry juice
hard ice cubes

Garnish: sprigs of mint or apple fans

Method:
Fill the glasses with ice. Pour in the vodka, elderflower cordial and the juices, stir and garnish with a sprig of mint or an apple fan.

Sea Breeze

The classic Sea Breeze is a gentle, easy drinking example of the 'strong, sweet, sour and weak' principle of cocktails, and is a favourite with drinkers all over the world.

2 Highball glasses

100ml vodka, try Smirnoff Penka
100ml cranberry juice
100ml pink grapefruit juice
hard ice cubes

Garnish: lime wedges

Method:
Fill the 2 glasses with ice, add the vodka and the rest of the juices and garnish with a wedge of lime.

Orange Breeze

Making your own orange vodka is easy: dry out the peeled zest of 2 oranges in a very slow oven, or on a radiator, then feed them into a nearly full bottle of vodka, add 20ml of gomme syrup, shake and leave for a few days.

2 Highball glasses

100ml Grey Goose orange vodka (or your homemade orange vodka)
120ml cloudy apple juice
100ml cranberry juice
hard ice cubes

Garnish: orange slices

Method:
Fill the glasses with ice, pour in the vodka and the juices, stir and garnish with orange slices.

Bay Breeze

The Sea Breeze's laid-back, tropical cousin, and a perfect drink for the beach.

2 Highball glasses

100ml Wyborowa pineapple vodka
120ml cranberry juice
100ml fresh pineapple juice
hard ice cubes

Garnish: pineapple slices

Method:
Fill the glasses with ice, pour in the drinks and stir. Garnish with a thin slice of pineapple.

Melon Breeze

Simple and very refreshing.

2 Highball glasses

100ml Wyborowa melon vodka
120ml cloudy apple juice
100ml cranberry juice
hard ice cubes

Garnish: melon slices, with the skin left on

Method:
Fill the glasses with ice, pour in the vodka and the juices, stir and garnish with a melon slice.

Jamaican Breeze

A terrific summer drink, invented by one of the LAB barstaff, and a good alternative to Pimm's.

2 Highball glasses

75ml Sailor Jerry Spiced Caribbean rum or Morgan Spiced rum
25ml vanilla liqueur
juice of 1 lime
150ml cloudy apple juice
hard ice cubes

Garnish: apple fans

Method:
Fill the glasses with ice. Shake all the ingredients in a Boston shaker and then pour over the ice and garnish with an apple fan.

Passionfruit Collins

If you don't want to use gomme syrup, you can make your own passionfruit purée (see p29) and add it instead.

2 Highball glasses

100ml vodka or gin
50ml lemon juice
flesh and seeds of 2 ripe passionfruit
4 teaspoons gomme syrup
soda (to top up)
crushed ice

Garnish: edible flowers and mint leaves

Method:
Half fill a Boston glass with crushed ice, and add the vodka or gin, lemon juice, passionfruit and gomme syrup. Stir well and split between 2 glasses. Top up with more ice almost to the rim, then with soda. Garnish with a flower and a few mint leaves.

Tom Collins

Nobody is quite sure who Mr Collins was, or even if he existed, but the first version is traditionally said to have been made with 'Old Tom', a once-popular sweetened London gin.

2 Highball glasses

100ml gin
50ml fresh lemon juice
25ml gomme syrup
soda (to top up)
crushed ice

Garnish: lemon twists and sprigs of mint

Method:
Half fill a Boston glass with crushed ice, add the gin, lemon juice and gomme syrup, stir and split between 2 glasses. Top up with more ice almost to the rim, then with soda. Garnish with lemon twists and mint.

Kiwi Fruit Collins

A great looking drink.

2 Highball glasses

1 peeled and diced ripe kiwi fruit
4 teaspoons gomme syrup
100ml vodka
50ml lemon juice
soda or 7-Up (to top up)
crushed ice

Garnish: kiwi fruit wheels

Method:
Muddle the kiwi fruit in a Boston glass with the gomme syrup and a little crushed ice. Half fill the glass with ice. Add the vodka and lemon juice, stir and split between the 2 glasses. Top up with more ice almost to the rim, then with soda or 7-Up, and garnish with kiwi fruit wheels.

Elderflower Collins

If you have some elderflowers to hand, they will make a perfect garnish.

2 Highball glasses

100ml gin
50ml lemon juice
25ml elderflower cordial
4 teaspoons gomme syrup
soda (to top up)
crushed ice

Garnish: elderflowers (optional)

Method:
Half fill a Boston glass with crushed ice, add the gin, lemon juice, elderflower cordial and gomme syrup, stir and split between the 2 glasses. Top up with more ice almost to the rim, then with soda.

Lemongrass Collins

To make your lemongrass vodka, bruise a stalk of lemongrass until soft and push it into a nearly full bottle of vodka. Leave for 3–4 days, shaking occasionally.

2 Highball glasses

80ml lemongrass-infused vodka
30ml gomme syrup
50ml lemon juice
soda or 7-up (to top up)
crushed ice

Garnish: lemongrass tubes, mint leaves and orange twists

Method:
Fill the glasses half way up with crushed ice. Add your vodka, gomme syrup and lemon juice and stir until well mixed. Top with more ice almost to the rim, then with soda or 7-Up and garnish.

Raspberry Collins

Chambord is a raspberry and blackberry liqueur from the Loire Valley in France. Instead of the Stolichnaya Razberi vodka you can use homemade raspberry vodka (see p29).

2 Highball glasses

14 raspberries
4 teaspoons gomme syrup
100ml Stolichnaya Razberi vodka
25ml Chambord
50ml lemon juice
soda or 7-Up (to top up)
crushed ice

Garnish: raspberries

Method:
Muddle the raspberries in a Boston glass with the gomme syrup and a little crushed ice. Half fill the glass with ice. Add the vodka, Chambord and lemon juice, stir and split between 2 glasses. Top up with more ice almost to the rim, then with soda or 7-Up, and garnish with 2 raspberries.

Lemongrass and Wild Chilli Martini

As with the Lemongrass Collins, you will need to make your own flavoured vodka. Bruise 2 stalks of lemongrass gently with a rolling pin, then stick them into a nearly full bottle of vodka with 25ml of gomme syrup and a red chilli which you have pricked all over with a fork. Screw the top back on, shake it gently, then leave the bottle for a week or so to let the flavours develop, shaking it, when you remember, to help things along. This is an ideal drink for a cold winter's evening.

2 Martini glasses, preferably frozen

100ml lemongrass and chilli vodka
25ml Manzana apple liqueur
50ml cloudy apple juice
juice 1/2 lemon
25ml gomme syrup
hard ice cubes

Garnish: small red chillies and lemongrass tubes

Method:
Put all the ingredients into a Boston shaker and shake hard. Fine-strain into glasses and garnish with lemongrass tubes and small, halved red chillies.

French Martini

This was very popular in the early 90s at the start of the cocktail revolution. It is a very elegant drink.

2 Martini glasses, preferably frozen

80ml Finlandia vodka
25ml Chambord (raspberry and blackberry liqueur)
12 raspberries
40ml fresh pineapple juice
10ml gomme syrup
hard ice cubes

Garnish: raspberries

Method:
Shake everything together in a Boston shaker, then fine-strain into the glasses.
Garnish with raspberries.

Pomegranate Martini

A delicious drink for the pomegranate season.

2 Martini glasses, preferably frozen

100ml Finlandia vodka
juice of 2 ripe pomegranates, seeds retained
4 teaspoons liquid from a jar of maraschino cherries
8 mint leaves
hard ice cubes

Garnish: pomegranate seeds

Method:
Squeeze the juice out of the pomegranates and retain a few of the seeds for the garnish. Shake all the ingredients together in a Boston shaker. Strain into the glasses and garnish with the seeds.

Raspberry Martini

Vibrantly coloured, sensational tasting and very moreish.

2 Martini glasses, preferably frozen

12 raspberries
50ml Chambord (raspberry and blackberry liqueur)
100ml vodka (Stolichnaya Razberi, or homemade raspberry-flavoured vodka – see p29)
hard ice cubes

Garnish: raspberries

Method:
Muddle the raspberries with the Chambord. Add the vodka and ice, then shake in a Boston shaker and fine-strain into the glasses. Garnish with a few raspberries.

Black Star Liner Martini

Named after a shipping line in Ghana, where my family comes from. It was set up many years ago by the Jamaican activist and visionary Marcus Garvey – hardly the last word in opulence nowadays but I think it deserves its own cocktail!

Patrón XO Café is a Mexican coffee-flavoured tequila.

2 Martini glasses, preferably frozen

50ml Mozart Chocolate liqueur
50ml freshly made espresso
50ml Patrón XO Café
2 teaspoons gomme syrup
hard ice cubes

Garnish: espresso beans and chocolate shavings

Method:
Shake all the ingredients in a Boston shaker and then strain into the 2 glasses. Add a few whole espresso beans and float chocolate shavings on the top

Basil and Pineapple Martini

I have used basil and strawberry before but then I saw a bartender using the combination of basil and pineapple and decided to experiment myself. Smirnoff Penka is a great new vodka, with a bottle cap that is ideal for measuring.

2 Martini glasses, preferably frozen

150g (5oz) pineapple, diced
20ml gomme syrup
12 basil leaves
100ml Smirnoff Penka vodka
1 tablespoon lemon juice
hard ice cubes

Method:
Muddle the pineapple with the basil and gomme syrup in a Boston glass, then add the vodka, lemon juice and ice. Shake, then fine-strain into the glasses.

Maverick Martini or Porn Star Martini

Named after a louche Cape Town night club I frequented while writing this book. The shot of Champagne on the side of the beautifully coloured passionfruit and vanilla Martini makes this is a very seductive drink. The first time I made these in Townhouse the whole bar was ordering them by the end of the night.

2 Martini glasses, preferably frozen, and tall shot glasses for Champagne on the side

80ml Cariel Vanilla Vodka
15ml Passoa (passionfruit liqueur)
flesh and seeds of 4 passionfruit
5 teaspoons vanilla sugar
100ml Champagne
1 passionfruit, halved
hard ice cubes

Method:
Shake all the ingredients except the Champagne, the halved passionfruit and 1 teaspoon of vanilla sugar in a Boston shaker, and then strain into glasses. Separately, pour out 2 glasses of Champagne and dust the halved passionfruit with the remaining sugar. Dunk the passionfruit in the Martini glasses, with spoons: the idea is to fish out the fruit, eat it with the spoon, drink the Champagne and then enjoy the cocktail at leisure.

Blanc Martini

This was on the original menu at LAB the first year it opened. It is a great drink and easy to make at home.

2 Martini glasses, preferably frozen

75ml Finlandia vodka
25ml white crème de cacao
1 tablespoon coconut cream (Coco Lopez)
50ml single cream
hard ice cubes

Garnish: coconut flakes

Method:
Shake all the ingredients in a Boston shaker and strain. Garnish with coconut flakes.

Watermelon Martini

This is at present the darling of the London cocktail scene. A must-have at Townhouse.

2 Martini glasses, preferably frozen

6 chunks of watermelon, about 2.5cm (1in) cubes
25ml gomme syrup
100ml Finlandia vodka
hard ice cubes

Garnish:watermelon slices, with the skin left on

Method:
Bash the watermelon with the gomme syrup in a Boston glass, and add the ice and vodka. Shake and then fine-strain. Serve, garnished with a watermelon slice on the rim of the glass.

Elderflower Martini

Ciroc vodka is a grape-based vodka from France. I used it because it was new to the market and a bit obscure. It is a very unusual tasting vodka and the grape and elderflower work well together. If you don't have Ciroc you could add a couple of grapes to 50ml vodka and shake it in a Boston shaker; otherwise just use good vodka.

2 Martini glasses, preferably frozen

50ml Ciroc vodka
50ml Tanqueray no.10 gin
25ml gomme syrup
40ml fresh lemon juice
2 teaspoons grated fresh ginger
25ml elderflower cordial
hard ice cubes

Method:
Shake all the ingredients in a Boston shaker, then fine-strain into the glasses.

Passionfruit Martini

Passoa is a coral-red passionfruit liqueur made by Cointreau in Spain. It has a fresh scent of passionfruit and citrus.

2 Martini glasses, preferably frozen

100ml Finlandia or Ketel One vodka
flesh and seeds of 4 ripe passionfruit
25ml Passoa (optional)
hard ice cubes

Garnish: passionfruit halves dusted with icing sugar.

Method:
Shake all the ingredients together in a Boster shaker and strain. Garnish with half
a passionfruit.

Morris Major

A frosty version of a hot toddy, shaken, not stirred, to distribute the honey evenly. Named after a legendary Cape Town socialite and bon viveur. For vanilla-infused bourbon split 2 fresh vanilla pods in half and insert into a nearly full bottle of bourbon and leave for 4–5 days.

2 Martini glasses, preferably frozen

100ml vanilla-infused bourbon
2 tablespoons runny honey (acacia honey if possible)
50ml lemon juice
1 tablespoon vanilla sugar
dash of Angostura bitters (optional)
hard ice cubes

Garnish: lemon slices

Method:
Shake all the ingredients together in a Boston shaker and strain. Garnish with lemon slices.

Parma Violet

My childhood love of sweets strikes again... This could be served either straight up in Martini glasses, or on the rocks in Old-fashioned glasses. If you can find a packet of Parma violet sweets, grind a few up and sprinkle them on top.

2 Martini glasses, preferably frozen or
Old-fashioned glasses

75ml Finlandia vodka
25ml Archer's peach schnapps
20ml violet liqueur (Crème Yvette)
50ml lemon juice
20ml gomme syrup
12 drops of orange bitters
hard ice cubes

Garnish: edible flowers

Method:
Shake all the ingredients in a Boston shaker and fine-strain into the 2 glasses and garnish.

Lab and Townhouse drinks made easy

The two London bars I own have pioneered hundreds of new cocktails over the years, and – from the number of bar menus that go walkabout every week! – I suspect that customers would like to reproduce some of them at home. LAB stands for London Academy of Bartending which I founded and Townhouse is situated in a classic town-house on Beauchamp Place.

Some of the recipes are very simple – the Bramble, for instance – while others call for a few exotic ingredients which you probably don't have at home. Find a recipe that everyone likes, however, and you will be surprised how quickly you can go through a bottle of limoncello or pineapple vodka.

Three Berry Daiquiri

This is a good summer alternative to other daiquiris when these fruits are in season.

2 Tall goblets, sugar-rimmed

100ml Bacardi 8-year old rum
25ml Chambord (raspberry and blackberry liqueur)
50ml lemon juice
1 tablespoon gomme syrup
4 strawberries
8 raspberries
8 blackberries
crushed ice

Garnish: strawberries, raspberries and blackberries speared on toothpicks

Method: In an electric blender, whizz all the ingredients together for 45 seconds and pour into the goblets. Garnish with the speared fruit.

Bramble

Crème de mûre is one of the best of a range of fruit liqueurs traditionally made around Dijon, in Burgundy. It has a haunting aroma of wild blackberries, and makes a very acceptable alternative to crème de cassis (blackcurrant) in a Kir or a Kir Royale.

2 Highball glasses

100ml Plymouth or Tanquerey No.10 gin
50ml lemon juice
50ml gomme syrup
25ml crème de mûre
crushed ice

Garnish: blackberries

Method: Half fill the highballs with crushed ice. Add the gin, lemon juice and gomme syrup and stir both drinks. Add more crushed ice and crown with a float of crème de mûre, gently poured over the back of a spoon. Garnish with a few blackberries.

Jadoo

I was commissioned to create a cocktail list for an upmarket Indian bar and restaurant opening in Soho, London.

Seeking inspiration from the days of the Raj, I decided to base it on gin and tonic – probably the most popular drink with the colonials and their memsahibs at that time. In addition to being a great mixer for gin, quinine flavoured tonic water was effective against malaria. I also used mint, a favourite herb in India, and modestly named it Jadoo – Hindi for 'magic'.

2 Old-fashioned glasses

12 mint leaves
1 lime, diced
1 tablespoon caster sugar
100ml Bombay Sapphire gin
tonic water (to top up)
crushed ice

Garnish: sprigs of mint

Method: Muddle the mint, lime and sugar together in the glasses, then half fill with crushed ice. Add the gin and stir. Add more ice and top up with tonic. Garnish with a sprig of mint.

Bon-bon

This cocktail takes me back to my childhood – and my unhealthy fondness for sweets. With its mix of vanilla vodka, butterscotch schnapps and limoncello, this cocktail might stretch the resources of your cocktail cabinet a little, but, for any grown-up kids, it's worth it. Usually served in Martini glasses, but can also be served on the rocks in Old-fashioned glasses.

2 Martini glasses, preferably frozen, or Old-fashioned glasses

100ml Cariel vanilla vodka or homemade vanilla vodka (see p29)
25ml Teichenné butterscotch schnapps
50ml limoncello
50ml lemon juice
1 tablespoon vanilla sugar
hard ice cubes

Garnish: lemon fans

Method: Shake everything together in a Boston shaker and strain into the glasses. Garnish, if you like, with lemon sweets ground to a coarse powder or a lemon fan.

El Presidente Julep

I wanted a South American name for this cocktail, and a Duran Duran song inspired me to call it El Presidente.

2 large Old-fashioned glasses

12 mint leaves
2 tablespoons vanilla sugar
100ml Bacardi 8 year old rum
crushed ice

Garnish: mint leaves

Method: Bash the mint and sugar together, half in each glass, then half fill with crushed ice. Add the rum, stir, then fill to the rim with more crushed ice. Garnish with a few mint leaves.

Chelsea Rose

The perfect drink for a tipple at the Chelsea Flower Show. This cocktail overflows with the aromas and flavours of an English summer: hedgerows, orchards and cucumber sandwiches. Hendrick's gin is actually flavoured with cucumber, and also has a distinct aroma of rose petals.

2 Highball glasses

100ml Hendrick's gin
25ml elderflower cordial
100ml cloudy apple juice, mixed with
1 tablespoon raspberry purée (see p29)
hard ice cubes

Garnish: apple fans and edible flowers

Method: Fill the glasses with ice cubes, then add all the ingredients and stir gently. Garnish with an apple fan and a flower.

Loretto Lemonade

Named after the town in Kentucky where Maker's Mark is distilled, a true place of pilgrimage for all bourbon aficionados.

2 Highball glasses

75ml Maker's Mark bourbon
25ml Midori (melon liqueur)
1 teaspoon gomme syrup
juice of 1 lime
100ml cloudy apple juice
100ml ginger beer
hard ice cubes

Method: Half fill each glass with ice, then add the bourbon, Midori, gomme syrup and fruit juices. Stir well, fill up with ice and top up with ginger beer.

Coleraine Cooler

Invented by one of my barmen at LAB; surprisingly enough, he is from Coleraine, Ireland. It is one cocktail I wish I had invented.

2 Highball glasses

10 mint leaves
1 tablespoon vanilla sugar
25ml lime juice
100ml Zubrowka (bison grass vodka)
25ml Manzana apple liqueur
100ml cloudy apple juice
25ml Goldschlager (cinnamon schnapps with gold leaf)
crushed ice

Garnish: apple fans dusted with cinnamon and sprigs of mint

Method: Half fill the glasses with crushed ice, add the mint, sugar and lime juice, then stir and gently bruise the mint. Add the vodka, the Manzana and the apple juice and stir. Add more ice and top with the Goldschlager, floated over the back of a spoon. Garnish with an apple fan and a sprig of mint.

Forbidden Fruit

This drink is a sort of high-octane Moscow Mule: Tanqueray No.10, the base spirit, is distilled with fresh botanicals rather than the usual dried juniper berries, orris root and the rest, giving it a distinctively fresh aroma.

2 Highball glasses

2 strawberries, finely diced
4 blackberries
4 raspberries
1 tablespoon vanilla sugar
50ml lime juice
100ml Tanqueray No.10 gin
20ml Chambord (optional)
ginger beer (to top up)
crushed ice

Garnish: slices of strawberry, blackberries and raspberries on toothpicks and mint leaves

Method: In a Boston glass, muddle the fruit with the sugar, lime juice and a little crushed ice, and pour half in each glass. Half fill the glasses with crushed ice, add the gin and Chambord (if using) and stir. Add more crushed ice, nearly to the brim, and top up with ginger beer. Garnish with the speared fruit and a few mint leaves.

Markee

My favourite bourbon cocktail, created by a friend when we first opened LAB.

2 Highball or Old-fashioned glasses

75ml Makers Mark bourbon
25ml Chambord (raspberry and blackberry liqueur)
50ml lemon juice
12 raspberries
100ml cranberry juice
2 teaspoons gomme syrup
hard ice cubes
crushed ice

Method: Fill both glasses with crushed ice. Shake all the ingredients together in a Boston shaker, fine-strain and pour over the crushed ice.

Rapaska

An ideal drink for brunch created by my friend
Jamie Terrell. As an alternative to Stolichnaya
Razberi vodka, you can make your own
raspberry vodka (see p29).

2 Highball glasses

80ml Stolichnaya Razberi vodka
20 raspberries
100ml cloudy apple juice
20ml gomme syrup
120ml fresh orange juice
2 whole passionfruit
hard ice cubes

Garnish: 2 raspberries and sprigs of mint

Method: Shake all the ingredients in a Boston
shaker. Strain over crushed ice and garnish
with a raspberry and a sprig of mint.

Spiced Swizzle

One of the first drinks I ever created as a
bartender, and very simple to make at home.

2 Highball or Old-fashioned glasses

100ml Sailor Jerry Spiced rum or Morgan
Spiced rum
1 tablespoon gomme syrup
50ml lime juice
25ml amaretto Disaronno
crushed ice

Garnish: lime wheels and twists

Method: Half fill the glasses with crushed ice,
add the rum, gomme syrup and lime juice
and stir. Fill up with ice, almost to the rim and
top with a float of amaretto. Garnish with lime.

Jamboree

Not a drink for boy scouts, but a traditional Easter favourite for the crowd at Townhouse, who always seem to assemble for a celebratory tipple at that time of year.

2 Old-fashioned glasses

75ml Wyborowa pineapple vodka
25ml Licor 43 (cuarenta y tres)
flesh and seeds of 4 passionfruit
1 ripe mango, peeled, stoned and puréed
juice of $1/2$ lemon
crushed ice
hard ice cubes

Garnish: passionfruit and mint leaves

Method: Fill the glasses with crushed ice. Shake everything else together in a Boston shaker with the hard ice cubes, fine-strain and pour over the crushed ice. Garnish with half a passionfruit and a few mint leaves.

Kentucky Iced Tea

Iced tea, while hugely popular in the USA and most of Europe, has never really taken off in Britain. Perhaps it just needs a helping hand…

2 Highball glasses

75ml bourbon (ideally Buffalo Trace)
25ml vanilla liqueur
50ml lemon juice
4 teaspoons vanilla sugar
12 mint leaves
iced tea (to top up), use Liptonice, or make your own)
crushed ice
hard ice cubes

Garnish: mint leaves

Method: Fill the glasses with crushed ice, then shake together all the ingredients except the tea in a Boston shaker. Strain into the glasses and top up with tea and garnish with a few mint leaves.

Rich Dogg

The 'Rich' in this cocktail is my friend Richard Hargroves, and the 'Dogg' – well, I'll let you guess.

2 Martini glasses, frozen and sugar-rimmed

2 teaspoons grated fresh ginger
10 white or black grapes
3 teaspoons caster sugar
80ml Ciroc vodka (grape-based vodka from France)
30ml Passoa (passionfruit liqueur)
flesh and seeds of 2 passionfruit
25ml lemon juice

Garnish: 2 grapes

Method: In the glass half of a Boston shaker, bash together the ginger, grapes and sugar. Add the remaining ingredients, shake very hard and fine-strain into the glasses. Garnish with a grape, slightly cut so you can slide it onto the rim of the glass.

Sky Cruiser

I received a bottle of peach vodka from a friend and created this cocktail, but couldn't find a name for it, so kept it in my diary. Then I flew to Japan and the plane was called Sky Cruiser – perfect.

2 Martini glasses, preferably frozen

80ml Stolichnaya peach vodka
30ml Licor 43 (cuarenta y tres)
50ml lemon juice
20ml passionfruit syrup
hard ice cubes

Method: Shake all the ingredients in a Boston shaker and fine-strain into glasses.

La Cucaracha

Sometimes, drinks just have a name that seems to suit them. La Cucaracha is not an exotic Spanish dance, it's a cockroach – but it sounds good! Tequila is a difficult spirit to blend with other flavours, but this time I think I hit the spot.

Agavero is tequila-based liqueur, named after the agave cactus.

2 Highball glasses

75ml Jose Cuervo Tequila Especial
25ml Agavero
40ml lime juice
flesh and seeds of 2 passionfruit
100ml cloudy apple juice
4 teaspoons vanilla sugar
crushed ice
hard ice cubes

Garnish: sprigs of mint

Method: Fill the glasses with crushed ice. Shake all the ingredients together in a Boston shaker, strain and pour over the crushed ice. Garnish with a sprig of mint.

Black Bison

Zubrowka is a bison grass flavoured vodka. Bison grass only grows wild in eastern Poland, and gives the vodka a unique taste.

2 Highball glasses

8 blackberries
1 tablespoon caster sugar
20ml lemon juice
100ml Zubrowka (bison grass vodka)
20ml Chambord (raspberry and blackberry liqueur)
120ml cloudy apple juice
crushed ice

Garnish: blackberries and apple fans

Method: In a mixing glass, bash together the blackberries, sugar and lemon juice with a scoop of crushed ice. Stir in the Zubrowka, Chambord and apple juice, and split between the 2 glasses. Top up with crushed ice, stir again, and garnish with a few blackberries and an apple fan.

Indian Summer

Use the rosewater you find in delicatessens, not at the cosmetics counter! Alternatively, crème de rose is a liqueur flavoured with rose petals. Both are highly perfumed, so use them wisely.

2 Highball glasses

10 raspberries
3 teaspoons caster sugar
2 teaspoons rosewater (or crème de rose)
100ml Plymouth gin
120ml cranberry juice
crushed ice

Garnish: raspberries and sprigs of mint

Method: In a mixing glass, bash the raspberries, caster sugar, rosewater and gin together with a scoop of crushed ice. Split between the 2 glasses, half fill with crushed ice, add the cranberry juice, stir thoroughly and top up with more ice. Garnish with raspberries and a sprig of mint.

Madagascar Sour

A sort of autumnal variation of a Lime Daiquiri, made with a very good aged rum and the delicious Xanath vanilla liqueur. Very popular at Townhouse, and named after the home of much of the world's vanilla. This is my favourite rum drink.

2 Martini glasses, preferably frozen

80ml Bacardi 8 year old rum
4 teaspoons vanilla sugar
50ml lime juice
25ml Xanath vanilla liqueur

Garnish: lime wheels

Method: Shake all the ingredients together in a Boston shaker, then fine-strain into the glasses. Garnish with a lime wheel.

Buena Vista Barfly

The classic drink Greyhound uses ordinary vodka and grapefruit. This twist on the original is simple, but delicious.

2 Old-fashioned glasses, sugar-rimmed

1 large pink grapefruit, peeled and cut into small chunks
4 teaspoons caster sugar
100ml Wyborowa melon vodka
crushed ice

Method: In a mixing glass, muddle the fruit with the sugar, then half fill with crushed ice, add the vodka, stir, add more crushed ice and stir again. Split between the 2 glasses.

Absolutely Crushed

This was on the first menu I created for LAB. The most outrageous mix of sweet and sour and one of my favourites.

Mandarin Napoléon is a Belgian liqueur made with fresh mandarine peels from Sicily macerated with cognac and distilled 3 times.

2 Highball glasses

4 kumquats, quartered
4 teaspoons soft brown sugar
flesh and seeds of 2 passionfruit
100ml Absolut Citron
40ml Mandarin Napoléon
20ml lemon juice
crushed ice

Garnish: 2 kumquats

Method: In a mixing glass, muddle the kumquats, sugar and passionfruit together with a little crushed ice. Split between the glasses and half fill them with crushed ice. Add the vodka and stir thoroughly. Fill up with crushed ice and gently crown with Mandarin Napoléon using the back of a barspoon. Garnish with kumquat halves.

Blackbird

Blackberry and apple is a wonderful autumnal combination, mixed here with the warm fragrance of vanilla.

2 Highball glasses

100ml Cariel vodka or homemade vanilla vodka (see p29)
8 blackberries
3 teaspoons caster sugar
20ml lemon juice
120ml cloudy apple juice
crushed ice

Garnish: blackberries and sprigs of mint

Method: In a mixing glass, bash the vodka, blackberries, sugar and lemon juice together with a scoop of crushed ice. Divide between the 2 glasses, half fill with crushed ice, then add the apple juice and stir thoroughly. Top up with more ice and garnish with blackberries and a sprig of mint.

Ma Cherie or Mon Cheri

A great cocktail for an indulgent occasion, like Christmas or Mother's Day. Anybody who likes liqueur chocolates will love this rich, fruity drink.

2 Highball glasses

100ml Finlandia cranberry vodka
25ml Cherry Heering (cherry liqueur)
50ml cherry purée (see p84)
35ml Mozart dark chocolate liqueur
25ml lemon juice
20ml gomme syrup
20ml soda water or 7-up (to top up)
crushed ice
hard ice cubes

Garnish: orange twists and sprigs of mint

Method: Pour the vodka, Cherry Heering, cherry purée, chocolate liqueur, lemon juice and gomme syrup into a mixing glass, and stir well with hard ice cubes.

Half fill each glass with crushed ice, split the drink between the 2, stir, fill up with crushed ice and top up with soda or 7-Up. Stir again gently to mix all the ingredients and garnish with orange twists and a sprig of mint.

Monarch

A drink conceived in 2002 while I was trying to come up with new drinks for Townhouse. This creation was inspired by the Queen's Golden Jubilee that year; as I walked through Green Park the week before I thought about what was quintessentially English. Featuring her late mother's favourite tipple, gin, this is my favourite gin drink and I'm very proud of it. It's best to give the glasses an hour in the freezer first.

2 Martini glasses, preferably frozen

100ml Plymouth gin
25ml elderflower cordial
50ml lemon juice
4 teaspoons gomme syrup
8–10 drops peach bitters (optional)
8 mint leaves
hard ice cubes

Garnish: lemon twists (optional)

Method: Shake all the ingredients in a Boston shaker, fine-strain into the glasses and garnish with a twist of lemon if you like.

Rumba

I made this drink with a bizarre vanilla liquer but didn't think it was perfect, until Xanath came onto the market, which totally changed the flavour and made the drink amazing.

2 Old-fashioned glasses

80ml Appleton VX rum
20ml Xanath vanilla liqueur
2 tablespoons Greek yogurt
100ml cloudy apple juice
1 tablespoon vanilla sugar
hard ice cubes

Garnish: apple fans dusted with cinnamon

Method: Fill both glasses with ice, then shake all the ingredients together in a Boston shaker and split between the 2 glasses. Garnish with an apple fan.

Kool Hand Luke

My friend Jamie Terrell invented this drink so I have named it after his son Luke. Paul Newman would probably drink it with hard-boiled eggs.

2 Highball glasses

2 fresh limes, quartered
4 teaspoons soft brown sugar
8 drops Angostura bitters
100ml Myers's rum
crushed ice

Method: In a mixing glass, muddle the limes, sugar and Angostura bitters together with a little crushed ice. Divide between the 2 glasses and half fill each with crushed ice. Add the rum; stir, then fill up with more crushed ice and stir again.

Ruby Tuesday

Probably the most difficult drink to make in the world! Much easier to play on the guitar. There are just so many ingredients and the balance must be just right, but the finished product is incredible. This is the drink to have at Townhouse.

If you can't find cherry purée, stone 25 ripe cherries and blend them with a little gomme syrup, or use 40ml blended tinned cherries.

2 Martini glasses, preferably frozen or Old-fashioned glasses

80ml Finlandia Cranberry vodka
20ml Midori (melon liqueur)
20ml Mandarin Napoléon (orange liqueur)
20ml Licor 43 (cuarenta y tres)
20ml lemon juice
30ml cranberry juice
flesh and seeds of 2 passionfruit
40ml cherry purée
20ml passionfruit syrup
4 x 2cm (3/4in) cubes of watermelon
hard ice cubes
crushed ice (if serving in Old-fashioned glasses)

Method: Shake all the ingredients in a Boston shaker, or preferably a tin shaker (to ensure all the ingredients fit). Shake until well mixed and strain into the glasses.

Queen of Bahia

This drink is named for a very attractive Brazilian waitress!

2 Old-fashioned glasses

2 fresh limes, chopped in 12 half wedges
4 fresh strawberries
2 tablespoons dark soft brown sugar
100ml cachaça (sugar cane spirit)
25ml crème de fraise
crushed ice

Garnish: strawberry fans dusted with icing sugar

Method: In a mixing glass, muddle the limes and strawberries together with the sugar, and split between the 2 glasses. Add cachaça to both, half fill with crushed ice, stir and fill up with ice. Crown with a dribble of crème de fraise. Garnish with a strawberry fan.

Bisonite

Zubrowka and apple juice is a Polish classic: this is a refined version.

2 Martini glasses

100ml Zubrowka (bison grass vodka)
40ml cloudy apple juice
30ml passionfruit syrup
2 drops of peach bitters (optional)
10ml lemon juice
hard ice cubes

Garnish: apple fans

Method: Shake all the ingredients in a Boston shaker, then fine-strain into the glasses. Garnish with an apple fan.

Metropolis

I created this for the Absolut Mandrin launch in London.

2 Old-fashioned glasses

75ml Absolut Mandrin
25ml Mandarin Napoléon (orange liqueur)
50ml lemon juice
20ml gomme syrup
hard ice cubes

Garnish: orange twists

Method: Fill both glasses with ice cubes, then shake all the ingredients in a Boston shaker, strain and divide between the glasses. Garnish with twists of orange.

Very Berry

This is a bestseller at LAB.

2 Old-fashioned glasses

1 fresh lime, cut into 12 half wedges
12 blackberries
2 tablespoons caster sugar
100ml vodka
25ml crème de mûre
crushed ice

Method: Put the lime in a mixing glass with the blackberries, sugar and vodka and muddle all the ingredients together. Split between the 2 glasses, add half the crushed ice and stir. Top up each glass with crushed ice. Gently crown the finished cocktails with the crème de mûre, and serve.

Vitamina

A perfect revitalising drink for a Sunday afternoon. An alternative to a Virgin or Bloody Mary – if you want vodka add about 75ml for the 2 glasses.

2 Highball glasses

150ml fresh carrot juice
2 teaspoons celery salt
2 teaspoons Worcestershire sauce
2 teaspoons lemon juice
6 drops Tabasco
hard ice cubes

Garnish: carrot and
cherry tomatoes

Method: In a mixing glass, stir everything together with hard ice cubes. Pour into the glasses and garnish with long shavings of carrot and cherry tomatoes.

Honey Caipirinha

Perfect for the cocktail fan who wants to avoid refined sugar: in fact, any Caipirinha or Caipiroska recipe works very well with honey instead of gomme syrup or sugar.

2 Old-fashioned glasses

1 lime, cut into 12 half wedges
40ml runny honey
100ml cachaça (sugar cane spirit)
crushed ice

Method: Muddle the lime and honey together in a mixing glass, then add a scoop of crushed ice and the cachaça. Stir thoroughly and divide between the 2 glasses. Add more crushed ice to top up and then stir again.

Mango Caipirinha

An exotic twist on a classic.

2 Old-fashioned glasses

1 lime, cut into 12 half wedges
3–4 slices ripe mango
1 tablespoon caster sugar
100ml cachaça (sugar cane spirit)
crushed ice

Garnish: mango fans

Method: Muddle the lime, mango and sugar
together in a mixing glass, then add a scoop
of crushed ice and the cachaça. Stir
thoroughly and divide between the 2 glasses,
adding more crushed ice to top up and then
stir again. Garnish with a mango fan.

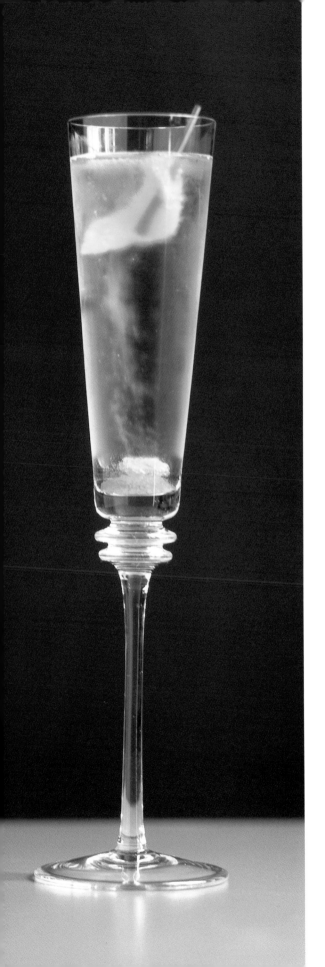

Champagne Cocktail

This is my favourite Champagne Cocktail.

Licor 43 (cuarenta y tres) is a bright yellow Spanish liqueur made from citrus and fruit juices, flavoured with vanilla and other aromatic herbs and spices, apparently, with 43 different ingredients in total.

2 Champagne flutes

1 small orange, peeled and carefully cut into skinless segments
10ml Licor 43 (cuarenta y tres)
4 drops orange bitters
2 white sugar cubes
30ml Woodford Reserve bourbon
Champagne (to top up)

Method: Marinate the orange segments in the Licor 43 for an hour or so. Drip 2 drops of bitters on each sugar cube, put 1 in each glass and carefully split the bourbon between the 2 glasses.

Almost fill the glasses with Champagne and drop a marinated orange segment into each glass.

Classic and Neo-Classic Cocktails

Many classic cocktails date from the turn of the 20th century, when ingredients were very limited. Gin, rum, whisky or brandy would simply be mixed with whatever was available to the bartender: often just sugar, ice and lemon juice.

As communications improved and the world grew smaller, cocktails became much more inventive. Ideas and ingredients spread around the globe: nowadays, new and exciting drinks are within everybody's grasp, and even the average supermarket will stock everything you need to make great drinks at home.

Bloody Mary

This drink was created at Harry's New York Bar in Paris in the early 1920s. This is the quintessential vodka cocktail and my favourite vodka classic. The point of a Bloody Mary is to invigorate, not to send you back to bed, so it should never be mind-numbingly strong. Nor does it need dozens of ingredients: Worcestershire sauce and lemon juice are all the tomato and vodka really need.

2 Highball glasses

75ml vodka, Ciroc (grape-based vodka from France) for preference
2 tablespoons Worcestershire sauce
2 teaspoons Tabasco (optional)
1 teaspoon celery salt
juice $1/2$ lemon
200ml tomato juice
hard ice cubes

Garnish: celery stick s and cherry tomatoes.

Method: Fill each glass with ice, then add the rest of the ingredients, stirring all the time. Garnish with a celery stick and a couple of cherry tomatoes.

Japanese Slipper

This classic uses Midori, the curious and distinctive bright green melon liqueur from Japan.

2 Martini glasses, preferably frozen

40ml Midori
80ml Jose Cuervo Especial tequila
40ml lime juice
60ml fresh pineapple juice
hard ice cubes

Method: Shake all the ingredients in a Boston shaker and strain into glasses.

Caipiroska

The vodka-based version of a Caipirinha.

2 Old-fashioned glasses

2 limes, each cut in 12 half wedges
2 tablespoons caster sugar
100ml vodka
crushed ice

Method: In a mixing glass, muddle the limes together with the sugar, then split them between the 2 glasses. Half fill each glass with crushed ice, add the vodka, stir, top up with ice and stir again.

Caipirinha

A favourite peasant drink in Brazil, where cachaça – a sugar cane spirit – is cheap and mostly, to be frank, rather crudely made. However, the new popularity of Caipirinhas has led to some much better cachaças being distilled.

2 Old-fashioned glasses

2 limes, each cut in 12 half wedges
2 tablespoons caster sugar (or soft brown sugar)
100ml cachaça
crushed ice

Method:In a mixing glass muddle the limes together with the sugar, then split between the 2 glasses. Half fill each glass with crushed ice, add the cachaça, stir, top up with ice and stir again.

Caipirinha for 6 people

6 Old-fashioned glasses

400ml cachaça
100ml gomme syrup
150ml freshly pressed lime juice
2 tablespoons caster sugar
hard ice cubes

Method: Fill up a 40oz pitcher with hard cubed ice. Stir all the ingredients in the pitcher with a ladle, then serve over fresh, hard ice cubes.

Margarita

This classic tequila cocktail, named after a famous Texan socialite, is best made with a young, unwooded tequila. Freshly squeezed lime juice is essential.

2 Martini or Old-fashioned glasses, rimmed (or only half rimmed) with lime juice and salt

75ml tequila
25ml Cointreau
50ml lime juice
hard ice cubes
crushed ice (if serving in Old-fashioned glasses)

Garnish: lime wheels

Method: Shake all the ingredients in a Boston shaker and strain into the glasses and garnish with a wheel of lime.

Manhattan

A classic cocktail which can be served in three different ways – sweet, perfect or dry – depending on whether Italian sweet vermouth, French dry vermouth, or a mixture of the two is used.

The method is the same for all three: put all ingredients into a Boston shaker, shake with hard ice cubes, strain into glasses and garnish. Serve in Martini glasses, preferably frozen, although all three can be served on the rocks in Old-fashioned glasses if preferred.

Manhattan Sweet

100ml rye whiskey
20ml red vermouth
2 drops of Angostura bitters

Garnish: maraschino cherries

Manhattan Perfect

100ml rye whiskey
10ml red vermouth
10ml dry vermouth
2 drops Angostura bitters

Garnish: orange twists

Manhattan Dry

100ml rye whiskey
20ml dry vermouth
2 drops Angostura bitters

Garnish: lemon twists

Millionaire

A classic cocktail which merits a revival. It can be served straight up in a Martini glass or on the rocks in an Old-fashioned glass.

2 Martini glasses, preferably frozen and sugar-rimmed or Old-fashioned glasses

75ml Jack Daniels
1 teaspoon Grenadine
1 teaspoon gomme syrup
40ml lemon juice
hard ice cubes

Garnish: lemon wheels

Method: Shake everything together in a Boston shaker, then fine-strain into the glasses. Garnish with a lemon wheel.

Champagne Cocktail

The perfect way to start a celebration – Christmas morning springs to mind. Just don't have more than two!

2 Champagne flutes

6 drops Angostura bitters
2 white sugar cubes
25ml cognac
Champagne (to top up)

Method: Drip 3 drops of bitters onto each sugar cube, put 1 in each glass, split the cognac between each glass and top up with Champagne. Don't stir!

Mint Julep

The classic all-American cocktail. The sort of drink to sip on a humid afternoon on a verandah in the deep South, as the ceiling fan turns slowly and the cicadas chirrup.

Old-fashioned glasses

16 mint leaves
2 tablespoons caster sugar
100ml bourbon
crushed ice

Garnish: sprigs of mint

Method: In a mixing glass, muddle the mint leaves and sugar together with a little of the bourbon and some crushed ice, and split between the 2 glasses. Half fill each glass with crushed ice, add the rest of the bourbon, stir and top up with crushed ice. Garnish with a sprig of mint.

Rusty Nail

Drambuie's mix of Scotch, herbs and honey makes a particularly warming liqueur. This famous old cocktail is best served after a good dinner on a cold night. This is a great Father's Day drink.

Old-fashioned glasses

100ml Scotch whisky
50ml Drambuie
hard ice cubes

Method: Fill each glass with ice, then split the Scotch and Drambuie between them and stir until well mixed.

Screwdriver

This famous (and famously simple) cocktail relies entirely on the quality of the ingredients, especially the orange juice, which if possible should be pressed just before using, and fine-strained to remove any bits of pulp. This is a cocktail that benefits from being well mixed, which some bars just don't do. Legend has it that the name derives from a Texan oil man who stirred his drink with a screwdriver.

2 Highball glasses

100ml Ketel One vodka
200ml freshly pressed orange juice
hard ice cubes

Garnish: orange slices

Method: Fill each glass with ice, split the vodka between them and top up with fresh orange. Stir extremely well and garnish with an orange slice.

Mojito

Cuba's national drink, served everywhere in Havana and now popular all over the world. Very moreish, and not as acidic as Margaritas and Caipirinhas.

2 Old-fashioned glasses

1 fresh lime, cut into 12 half wedges
14 mint leaves
4 teaspoons caster sugar
100ml Havana Club 3 year-old rum or Bacardi 8-year old rum
soda water (to top up)
crushed ice

Garnish: sprigs of mint

Method: In a mixing glass, muddle together the lime with the mint, sugar and a little crushed ice, and split between the 2 glasses. Half fill each glass with crushed ice, stir, add the rum, stir again, then top up with crushed ice and soda. Garnish with a sprig of mint.

Mojito for 6 people

6 Old-fashioned glasses

350ml Havana Club 3 year-old rum or Barcadi 8-year old rum
150ml freshly pressed lime juice
100ml gomme syrup
2 tablespoons caster sugar
100ml soda water
20 mint leaves
2 whole limes, quartered
hard ice cubes

Method: Fill up a 40oz pitcher with hard ice cubes. Add all the ingredients and then stir with a ladle until well mixed. Pour into the glasses with fresh hard ice cubes.

Moscow Mule

2 Highball glasses

juice of 1 lime
100ml vodka
ginger beer (to top up)
hard ice cubes

Garnish: ginger slices and
sprigs of mint

Method: Half fill each glass
with ice cubes, add the lime
juice and vodka, stir, then fill
up each glass with ice and
top up with ginger beer.
Garnish with thinly sliced
ginger and a sprig of mint.

This cocktail was created in America when
Russian vodka began to be imported. The
quality of the ginger beer is vital here: for a
proper mule-kick, use a powerful variety: Idris
Hot is good, or, even better, Fentiman's
naturally brewed ginger beer, if you can find it.

Negroni

Invented in Florence, but popular everywhere, and a great standby in pubs and airport lounges, where all three components of the Negroni can usually be found. Punt e Mes is often used in place of red vermouth: you might also try Vya, from California, or the hard-to-find Noilly Prat red. It can also be served with soda in a highball.

2 Old-fashioned glasses

60ml Plymouth gin
40ml red vermouth
40ml Campari
hard ice cubes

Garnish: orange slices

Method: Fill each glass with ice cubes, stir all the ingredients together in a mixing glass, then pour over the rocks and garnish with orange slices.

Old Fashioned

A bartender's favourite – as long as the bar's not too busy – this is the one recipe in which making two drinks at once doesn't really work, so the ingredients below are for one.

1 Old-fashioned glass (naturally enough)

1 brown sugar cube
1 dash orange bitters
1 dash Angostura bitters
1 teaspoon soda water
50ml Woodford Reserve bourbon
hard ice cubes

Garnish: strip of orange zest

Method: A good Old Fashioned takes several minutes to make, and involves muddling the sugar, bitters and soda water together while adding bourbon and ice cubes: the sugar needs to be more or less dissolved before you can start adding ice. Do it patiently, and the drink will be clear and well balanced, with the orange zest adding the vital fragrance.

Sidecar

Perhaps sensibly named for a motorcycle's passenger, not the driver.

2 Martini glasses, preferably frozen

50ml Cognac or Remy Grand Cru
50ml Cointreau
50ml fresh lemon juice
1 teaspoon caster sugar
hard ice cubes

Method: Shake all the ingredients in a Boston shaker, then fine-strain into the glasses.

Tequila Sunrise

The most instantly recognisable cocktail in the world, with dark red Grenadine gently drifting into orange juice.

2 Highball glasses

100ml Jose Cuervo Especial tequila
200ml freshly pressed orange juice
10ml Grenadine
hard ice cubes

Garnish: orange slices and fresh cherries

Method: Fill both glasses with ice, pour in the tequila, add the orange and carefully float the Grenadine on top.

Silk Stocking

Or, in fact, a pair of stockings.

This was very popular in the 80s. I have reinvented it with a scoop of ice cream – it can be any flavour, but preferably raspberry.

2 Martini glasses

80ml Jose Cuervo Especial tequila
20ml Grenadine
40ml white crème de cacao
50ml single cream
2 teaspoons caster sugar
1 soft scoop raspberry ice cream
crushed ice

Garnish: raspberries and cinnamon dust

Method: Blend all the ingredients for 30 seconds or so, pour into the glasses and garnish with the raspberries and cinnamon dust.

White Russian

The two Russians, white and black, have been popular after-dinner cocktails for decades, especially before Bailey's and a host of similar cream liqueurs arrived. Both drinks can be served with a small scoop of ice cream on top: vanilla in the White Russian and chocolate or coffee in the Black Russian. You could even have them for dessert. You should use Russian vodka for these, naturally.

2 Old-fashioned glasses

50ml vodka
50ml Kahlua
100ml single cream
2 soft scoops vanilla ice cream
hard ice cubes

Method: Fill both glasses with ice, pour half the vodka in each, then add the Kahlua and cream and stir. Place the ice cream on top.

Black Russian

2 Old-fashioned glasses

80ml vodka
40ml Kahlua
2 soft scoops chocolate
or coffee ice cream
hard ice cubes

Method: Fill both glasses with ice, pour half the vodka in each, then add the Kahlua and stir. Place the ice cream on top.

West Indian Rum Colada

Based on the classic Pina Colada, but updated to get away from the drink's slightly dubious reputation. Tropical and deeply refreshing.

2 large wine glasses

100ml Bacardi Oro
50g fresh pineapple chunks
50ml coconut cream (Coco Lopez)
50ml single cream
4 drops Angostura bitters
2 pinches of salt
crushed ice

Method: Fill both glasses with crushed ice. Blend all the ingredients together with a scoop of crushed ice and pour into the 2 glasses.

Whisk(e)y Sour

Sours can be made with any dark spirit, and are the simplest versions of the strong, sweet, sour, weak cocktail equation. You can drink it straight up in a Martini glass or on the rocks in an Old-fashioned. My favourite whisky cocktail; use whichever brand you like best.

2 Martini, preferably frozen or Old-fashioned glasses

100ml Scotch/Rye/Irish/Bourbon
50ml lemon juice
4 teaspoons caster sugar
4 dashes Angostura bitters
hard ice cubes

Garnish: cherries and lemon twists

Method: Shake all the ingredients in a Boston shaker and strain into the glasses. Serve with a cherry and a lemon twist.

Famous drinks in bars and hotels

Cocktails taste even better if you drink them in the right place. These bars and hotels are synonymous with one particular drink. In most cases, the drink was created there; in the cast of Duke's Hotel, it is simply the best place in the world to enjoy a Martini.

Duke's Hotel, London

Perhaps the most famous cocktail of them all, with countless variations and plenty of attached myths and legends. Nobody can be sure who created it, but it is often credited to an Italian bartender working in New York during the early part of the 20th Century.

In London, the best Martini is at Duke's Hotel, in St James's. The bar manager serves 100 a day, all from a special trolley wheeled into the traditionally decorated bar.

The first documented Dry Martini recipe specified Plymouth Gin. It appeared in Stuart's *Fancy Drinks and How to Mix Them* in 1896.

A Martini has a lifespan of about 5 minutes. It needs to be ice cold to be enjoyed properly.

The Classic Martini

Glass	2 Martini glasses, preferably frozen
Ingredients	3 dashes of dry French vermouth
	150ml Plymouth Gin, frozen
	hard ice cubes (if the gin isn't frozen)
Garnish	2 stoned olives or twists of lemon
Method	Pour half the vermouth into each glass, turn them carefully so each glass is coated, then pour out any residue. If you are using frozen gin, simply pour it into the glasses; if it's not frozen, stir the gin with the ice in a mixing glass and strain into the martini glass. Garnish with the olives or lemon and drink before it warms up.

Raffles Hotel, Singapore

The Singapore Sling was created at Raffles Hotel at the turn of the 20th Century by Hainanese-Chinese bartender Mr Ngiam Tong Boon. Originally, the Singapore Sling was intended as a drink for ladies, hence the attractive pink colour.

The Singapore Sling

Glass	2 Highball glasses
Ingredients	75ml Bombay Sapphire gin
	50ml lemon juice
	Generous dash of gomme syrup
	100ml ginger ale
	25ml Cherry Heering (float)
	25ml Bénédictine (float)
	hard ice cubes
Garnish	lemon fans
Method	Fill both glasses with ice cubes. In a mixing glass, stir together the gin, lemon juice and gomme syrup, then split between the 2 glasses. Top up with ginger ale, and carefully float the 2 liqueurs on top. Garnish with a lemon fan.

Harry's Bar, Venice

This cocktail was created by Giuseppe Cipriani at Harry's Bar in Venice in 1948, and named after a painter, Giovan Battista Bellini, who had an exhibition of his work in Venice at the time. Harry's Bar also invented the dish carpaccio of beef, named after the Renaissance artist Vittore Carpaccio.

Should you ever visit Harry's Bar, sit at the bar: it's cheaper, the bar snacks are free, and you can admire the skill and longevity of the barmen as they top up dozens of glasses of white peach purée with Prosecco. Use a good, fizzy (spumante) Prosecco: Bisol is an excellent brand.

The Bellini

Glass	2 Champagne flutes
Ingredients	2 fresh peaches, stoned and chopped (white peaches if possible)
	25ml crème de pêche
	Prosecco or Champagne (to top)
Method	Blend the peaches with the crème de pêche. Strain and divide between the 2 glasses. Top up with Prosecco or Champagne, stir gently and serve.

El Floridita, Havana

Invented by an American engineer called Jennings Cox, while working in a mining town called Daiquiri, in Cuba. He normally drank gin, but his supply had run out and so he devised a cocktail based on the local rum.

El Floridita and the nearby Bodeguita del Medio are Havana's two most famous bars, partly because that ubiquitous drinker Ernest Hemingway frequented both establishments. Scrawled on the wall in Bodeguita is the legend "My mojito in Bodeguita, my daiquiri in Floridita": perhaps not the finest poetry Papa H ever wrote, but a useful *aide memoire* for the alcoholically challenged.

The Daiquiri

Glass	2 Martini glasses
Ingredients	100ml Havana Club rum
	50ml lime juice
	4 teaspoons caster sugar
	hard ice cubes
Garnish	wheels of lime
Method	Shake all the ingredients together in a Boston shaker, then fine strain into the glasses. Garnish with a lime wheel.

Trader Vics, Oakland

Originally made with a fine, golden, medium-bodied Jamaican rum from Kingston, with inspiration from a Havana barman. Returning to Oakland after a trip to Cuba, Trader Vic added fresh lime juice, flavoured and sweetened it with orange curacao and almond-flavoured orgeat syrup. The Mai Tai became hugely popular in his Oakland bar, and can now be enjoyed in Trader Vics bars all over the world.

This version is based on the original 1944 recipe.

Mai Tai

Glass	2 Old-fashioned glasses
Ingredients	100ml Wray and Nephew 17 year-old rum
	juice of 1 lime
	25ml orange curacao
	50ml orgeat syrup
	2 teaspoons gomme syrup
	crushed ice
	hard ice cubes
Garnish	sprigs of mint
Method	In a Boston shaker, shake the rum, lime, curacao, orgeat and gomme syrup together with hard ice cubes. Fill both glasses with crushed ice and fine-strain the drink between them. Stir and garnish with a sprig of mint.

Moneypenny

2 Highball glasses

20 fresh raspberries
flesh and seeds of 2 passionfruit
20ml gomme syrup
120ml cloudy apple juice
120ml orange juice
crushed ice

Garnish: apple fans, raspberries, and sprigs
of mint

Method: Gently muddle the raspberries,
passionfruit and gomme syrup together with
some crushed ice in a mixing glass and split
between the 2 glasses. Add more crushed ice
and the fruit juices, stir, fill up with ice and
garnish with an apple fan, raspberries and a
sprig of mint.

Holly Goodhead

2 Highball glasses

20 fresh raspberries
120ml cranberry juice
2 tablespoons vanilla sugar
2 tablespoons natural yogurt
crushed ice

Method: Fill both glasses with crushed ice,
blend the other ingredients together and split
between the 2 glasses.

May Day

2 Highball glasses

2 ripe peaches, stoned and roughly chopped
4 strawberries, diced
Flesh and seeds of 2 passionfruit
120ml cloudy apple juice
1 tablespoons caster sugar
2 teaspoons grated fresh ginger
crushed ice

Garnish: apple fans

Method: Blend all the ingredients together
with crushed ice and split between the
glasses. Garnish with an apple fan.

There's nothing wrong with giving children the taste for cocktails: without alcohol, naturally… and 'naturally' is the right word to describe this delicious, healthy, vitamin-packed drink: just don't let the grown-ups drink it all. Mind you, it's very good with a splash of dark rum, which makes it a Honey Rydes Again…

Honey Ryder

2 Highball glasses or large goblets

100ml fresh orange juice
flesh and seeds of 2 passionfruit
1 banana, skinned and roughly chopped
2 tablespoons natural yogurt
4 teaspoons honey (acacia for preference)
4 teaspoons Demerara sugar
crushed ice

To garnish: 6 slices of fresh ripe banana and grated nutmeg

Method: Blend everything together with a scoop of crushed ice. Fill the glasses with crushed ice and pour in the drink.

Cut the 3 slices of banana from edge to centre, dust them with grated nutmeg and carefully slide them over the rim of the glass. Drink with a straw.

Christmas Jones

A fizzy drink for the nuclear expert in *The World is Not Enough*.

2 Highball glasses

4 fresh strawberries
2 teaspoons caster sugar
150ml pineapple juice
7-Up (to top)
hard ice cubes

Garnish: slices of strawberry and sprigs of mint

Method: Blend the strawberries, sugar and pineapple juice together. Fill both glasses with ice, split between the 2 glasses and top up with 7-Up. Garnish with slices of strawberry and a sprig of mint.

Jinx

Halle Berry is my favourite Bond girl and this drink matches the colour of her bikini in *Die Another Day*.

2 Highball glasses

1 ripe mango, stoned,
skinned and chopped roughly
8 fresh raspberries
120ml cloudy apple juice
4 teaspoons vanilla sugar
2 tablespoons natural yogurt
crushed ice

Garnish: slices of mango
and sprigs of mint

Method: Fill both glasses with crushed ice, then blend all the ingredients together with a scoop of crushed ice and then pour into the glasses. Garnish with a slice of mango and a sprig of mint.

Kissy Suzuki

To make your own raspberry purée see page 29.

2 Highball glasses

50ml raspberry purée
50ml cranberry juice
150ml cloudy apple juice
7-Up (to top up)
crushed or cubed ice

Garnish: strawberries

Method: Half fill both glasses with ice cubes. In a Boston shaker, shake together the raspberry purée, cranberry juice and apple juice with ice cubes. Split between the 2 glasses, top up with 7-Up and garnish with strawberries.

Lupe Lamora

Pussy Galore

2 Highball glasses

1 ripe fresh pear, cored and cut into chunks
20 fresh raspberries
flesh and seeds of 2 passionfruit
100ml cloudy apple juice
4 teaspoons Demerara sugar
crushed ice

Garnish: raspberries and sprigs of mint

Method: Fill both glasses with ice, then blend
the fruit, juices and sugar together with a
scoop of crushed ice and split between the
glasses – you can fine-strain the drink to get
rid of the pips if you like. Garnish with raspberries and sprigs of mint.

A golden drink for the unforgettable bond girl
in *Goldfinger*.

2 Highball Glasses

60ml orange juice
60ml cloudy apple juice
1 fresh mango, skinned and chopped
1 tablespoons vanilla sugar
2 teaspoons grated fresh ginger
crushed ice

Garnish: apple fans

Method: Blend everything together with
crushed ice and split between the glasses.
Garnish with an apple fan.

A brightly coloured drink to go with her vibrant hair in *Diamonds are Forever*.

2 Highball glasses

1 fresh ripe banana, peeled and roughly chopped
1 fresh ripe mango, stoned, peeled and roughly chopped
flesh and seeds of 2 passionfruit
8 fresh raspberries
120ml cloudy apple juice
4 teaspoons vanilla sugar
2 tablespoons natural low-fat yogurt
crushed ice

Garnish: slices of mango and sprigs of mint.

Method: Blend all the ingredients together with a scoop of crushed ice and split between the glasses, straining if you want to. Garnish with slices of mango and a sprig of mint.

It's definitely worth investing in a bottle of real maple syrup for this drink: the cheaper flavoured corn syrups are tasteless by comparison.

2 Highball glasses

20ml Grenadine
caster sugar
12.5ml chocolate sauce
380ml milk
20ml maple syrup
crushed ice
hard ice cubes

Method: First, dampen the rim of each glass with a little Grenadine, and coat with caster sugar. Then carefully squirt chocolate sauce around the inside of each glass.

Fill each glass with crushed ice. In a Boston shaker, shake together the milk, Grenadine and maple syrup with hard ice cubes. Strain and split between the 2 glasses.

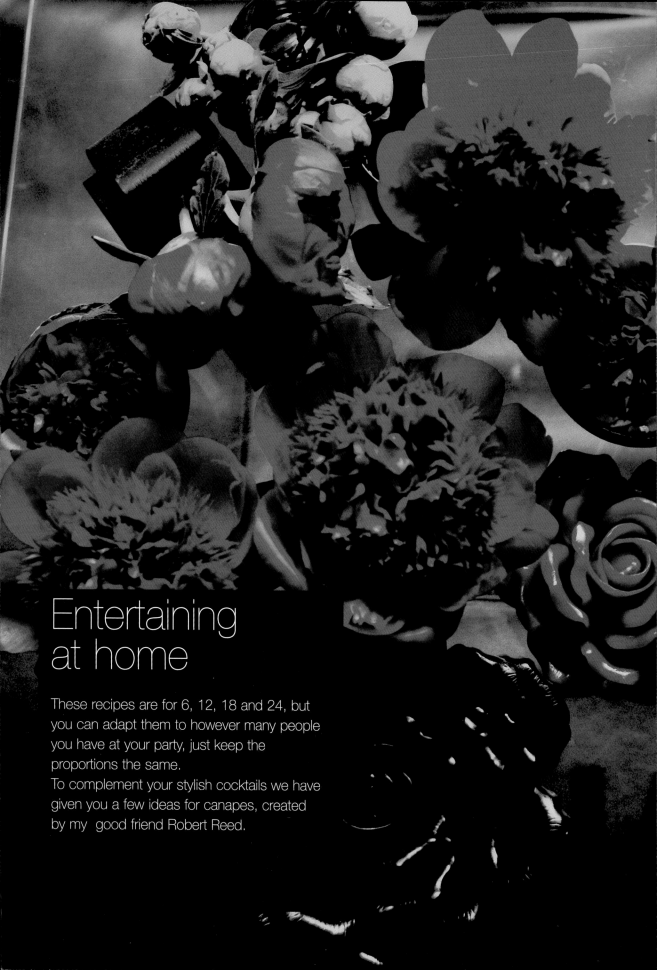

Entertaining at home

These recipes are for 6, 12, 18 and 24, but you can adapt them to however many people you have at your party, just keep the proportions the same.
To complement your stylish cocktails we have given you a few ideas for canapes, created by my good friend Robert Reed.

Cosmopolitan Punch

The success of *Sex and the City* has given this classic a new lease of life.

This is the perfect party drink: it's easy to make in a big punchbowl, and it actually benefits from being made the night before, so that the fruit can marinate in the alcohol. Remember to stick a few Martini glasses in the freezer; otherwise, you could serve it on the rocks in Old-fashioned glasses.

Serves 6

Glasses:	6 Martini glasses, preferably frozen
Ingredients:	2 whole oranges, diced
	6 whole limes, diced
	flesh and seeds of 4 passionfruit
	6 strawberries, quartered
	6 raspberries
	200ml Absolut Citron vodka
	90ml Cointreau
	60ml fresh lime juice
	150ml cranberry juice

Method: Put all the fruit into a punchbowl, pour in the vodka, Cointreau and juices and give it a gentle stir. Cover the bowl with cling film and put it in the fridge. When you're ready to serve it, give it another gentle stir and ladle it into glasses.

Bourbon Street Punch

When I worked at Smollensky's I used to make a Bourbon Street Breeze. I liked the name but wanted to make it into a punch and so added the warming flavours of vanilla, apples and raisins.

To infuse bourbon with raisins, simply push about 12 best quality, large raisins into the bottle and leave for 1–2 weeks, shaking occasionally.

This drink can be prepared several hours in advance.

Serves 12

Glass:	12 Old-fashioned glasses
Ingredients:	400ml raisin-infused Woodford Reserve bourbon
	250ml Grand Marnier
	100ml fresh lemon juice
	2 tablespoons caster sugar
	6 drops Angostura bitters
	2 litres pineapple juice
	hard ice cubes
Garnish:	orange twists
Method:	Mix everythng together in a punchbowl, taking care to dissolve the sugar. Serve on the rocks, garnished with orange twists.

West Indian Rum Punch

An intimidating list of ingredients, but actually very simple to make and a real crowd pleaser. Koko Canu is a coconut rum from Jamaica, if you don't have it, use Malibu instead.

This drink should be prepared 4–6 hours before serving so everything can marinate together.

Serves 18

Glass:	18 Old-fashioned glasses
Ingredients:	10 black peppercorns
	250ml Morgan Spice rum
	500ml Bacardi 8 year old
	250ml fresh lemon juice
	150ml Koko Kanu
	1 vanilla pod, split lengthways
	10 drops Angostura bitters
	4 tablespoons orange sorbet
	4 tablespoons caster sugar
	2 litres pineapple juice
	1 litre freshly pressed orange juice
	4 ripe mangoes, peeled, stoned and puréed, or 2 tinned mangoes blended with the canned syrup hard ice cubes
Garnish:	lemon, orange and lime slices, passionfruit, guava or any exotic fruit
Method:	Gently crack a few of the peppercorns. Mix everything together thoroughly in a large punchbowl and leave in the fridge. Stir again, and serve on the rocks, garnished with your chosen fruits.

Pimm's Royale

Pimm's is the classic drink of the English summer – in other words, usually consumed under the flap of a sodden marquee while rain lashes the cricket pitch. Originally made with 6 different spirit bases, now only the No. 1 (a gin base) and No. 6 (a vodka base) survive.

Serves 24

Glass: 24 Highball glasses
Ingredients: 300ml gin (preferably Bombay Sapphire)
2 bottles of Pimm's No. 1 Cup
1 punnet of fresh strawberries, quartered
1 punnet of fresh raspberries
1 punnet of fresh blackberries
1 punnet of fresh blueberries (optional)
1 large cucumber, sliced
1 small bunch of tarragon, chopped
6 large scoops of lemon or orange sorbet
3 tablespoons caster sugar
Champagne, Prosecco, or you can use Appletise, ginger ale or ginger beer (to top up)
hard ice cubes
Garnish: mint leaves
Method: Mix everything except the Champagne (or other fizz) together in a large jug (or use a couple), ladle on the rocks into glasses and top up with the fizz and garnish with mint.

Rare blackened beef with pesto

Fillet tails are cheaper than, but just as tender as, the rest of the fillet. Fillet of venison would work just as well.

4 beef fillet tails – about 200g (7oz) each – trimmed
1 tablespoon freshly milled black pepper
2 teaspoons coarse sea salt
100ml (3½fl oz) plum sauce (or apricot jam, warmed)
200ml (7fl oz) basil pesto

Dry the fillets with kitchen roll, then season liberally with black pepper and salt. Spread the beef lightly and evenly with plum sauce, then heat a grill pan or dry frying pan until smoking.

Sear the beef on all sides until it blackens – the sugar in the plum sauce helps the process – then rub the fillets liberally with pesto and leave to cool for 30 minutes.

To serve, slice the fillets fairly thinly and arrange on a wooden board or plate.

Seared sesame tuna with wasabi yoghurt dip

This Japanese inspired dish features wasabi, the fiercely hot green paste usually found on sushi and sahimi. Buy it in tubes, or buy the powder and make it yourself.

2 small loins blue fin tuna, about 400g (14oz) each
100g (3½oz) sesame seeds
150g (5oz) natural yogurt
25g (1oz) wasabi paste
few drops of sesame oil
1 teaspoon crushed garlic
coarse sea salt and black pepper

Season the tuna loins with salt and pepper, then press into the sesame seeds, making sure they are evenly coated.

In a hot non-stick frying pan, gently colour the tuna on all sides: this will take about 3 minutes. Leave at room temperature to cool.

Mix the yogurt, wasabi, sesame oil and garlic together. Just before serving, fold in a pinch of coarse sea salt to add a little crunch.

To serve, slice the tuna fairly thinly and arrange on a board or plate next to a pot of the wasabi yogurt.

Crostini

Crostini can be made from any good quality bread: slice a French stick thinly, spread the slices on oven trays, drizzle with olive oil and bake slowly until crisp and starting to brown, or slice ciabatta and grill it. Crunchy toppings work better on softer crostini; squishy toppings are more suited to crisp bases.

Onion, anchovy & black olive

A miniature version of *pissaladière*, the famous onion tart from Nice. Anchovies are optional.

4 medium onions, peeled and thinly sliced in
   half rings
2 tablespoons olive oil
1 tablespoon fresh thyme, chopped
10 anchovy fillets, halved lengthways
olive oil
10 black olives
salt and pepper

In a heavy based saucepan, gently cook the onions in the olive oil until soft and almost all the liquid has evaporated (about 45 minutes). The onions should just be starting to brown. Stir in the thyme, season with salt and pepper and leave to cool.

When cool, spread the onion mixture onto the crostini, then garnish with the anchovy strips in crosses and top with olive halves.

Parma ham & artichoke

Best on toasted ciabatta: roasted red peppers can be bought in jars if you don't want to roast and skin them yourself.

100g (3½oz) tapenade (black olive paste)
3 baby artichokes, quartered
10 thin slices of Parma ham
wild rocket to garnish
2 red peppers, grilled, skinned and cut
  into strips
olive oil

Spread the crostini with tapenade, top each with an artichoke quarter and a slice of ham, then garnish with a few leaves of rocket and strips of pepper. Drizzle with olive oil and serve.

Cherry tomato & basil

The marinating time is important here: the flavours and textures need a little time to meld together, but leave it too long and it will become too soggy.

500g (18oz) cherry tomatoes, halved
1 medium sized red onion, finely chopped
handful of basil leaves, shredded (reserve a
  few sprigs for garnish)
3 tablespoons olive oil
1 tablespoon lemon juice
1 teaspoon caster sugar
sea salt and coarse black pepper

Mix everything together in a bowl, leave to marinate for 10 minutes, then spoon the mixture onto the crostini. Garnish with basil sprigs and serve.

Baked new potatoes with caviar & cream cheese

An extravagant but classic combination of warm, nutty potatoes (Jersey Royals would be perfect), cool cream cheese and the world's priciest eggs. Superb with frozen vodka Martinis.

25–30 new potatoes
3 tablespoons olive oil
200g (7oz) cream cheese
1 tablespoon lemon juice
tabasco, to taste
3 tablespoons chives, chopped
60g (2$\frac{1}{2}$oz) Beluga caviar (Avruga or salmon eggs – keta – are cheaper!)
parsley
sea salt and black pepper

Preheat the oven to 180°C/350°F/gas 4. Roll the potatoes in oil, sprinkle with salt and bake them for 30 minutes, or until cooked. Set them aside in a warm place. Mix the cream cheese with the lemon juice and a dash of tabasco, season with salt and pepper and stir in the chives. Cut a lengthways slit in each potato, squeeze them to open, spoon a little cream cheese into each, top with caviar and serve with a few parsley leaves on top.

Grilled asparagus with San Daniele ham

This can be made with any good air-cured ham; Italian Parma ham or Spanish serrano ham would work just as well.

20 spears of large asparagus
(2 bunches)
2 tablespoons olive oil
juice and grated zest of 1 lemon
20 thin slices of San Daniele ham
salt and pepper

Trim the asparagus, using a potato peeler to pare any tough stalks. Cook them in boiling, salted water for about 4 minutes: they should be crunchy and bright green.

Refresh the asparagus in cold water (iced, if possible) and dry them with kitchen roll. On a heatproof dish, roll the spears in the oil until well coated, then put under a hot grill until they start to brown.

Remove them from the grill, add the lemon juice and zest, season with salt and pepper and leave to cool.

When cool, wrap each spear in a slice of ham and serve.

Crispy calamari with sweet chilli sauce

Very moreish. Thai sweet chilli sauce can be found in Oriental grocers and most supermarkets.

300g (10½oz) cleaned baby calamari, cut in half lengthways
1 egg, lightly beaten
150g (5oz) flour
1 teaspoon paprika
pinch of turmeric
1 teaspoon dried garlic flakes
pinch of cayenne pepper
2 teaspoons crushed black pepper
1 teaspoon coarse sea salt
1 litre sunflower oil
100ml Thai sweet chilli sauce
2 lemons, cut into wedges.

Heat the oil to 180°C.

Coat the calamari in the egg, then drain to remove any excess. Mix all the dry ingredients together, toss the calamari in the seasoned flour, shaking off any surplus, and immediately fry until crisp and golden. Drain briefly on scrunched-up kitchen roll, and serve with a pot of chilli sauce and lemon wedges.

walnut & stilton on chicory spoons

150g (5oz) Stilton cheese, at room temperature
20ml (1 1/2 tablespoons) ruby port
100g (3 1/2 oz) chopped walnuts
3 heads of chicory

Mash the Stilton and the port together with a fork and then fold in the chopped nuts.

Trim the roots of the chicory heads, peel off the outer leaves and discard, then drop the smaller, more tightly curled inner leaves straight into a bowl of iced water.

Just before serving, arrange the chicory 'spoons' on a serving plate and put a teaspoon of the cheese, port and nut mixture into each.